MESSAGES

NICKY HOLFORD

COLLINS
8 Grafton Street, London W1
1989

William Collins Sons & Co. Ltd
London · Glasgow · Sydney · Auckland
Toronto · Johannesburg

BRITISH LIBRARY CATALOGUING IN PUBLICATION DATA

Holford, Nicky
Messages.
823'.914 [F]

ISBN 0-00-223416-5

First published 1989
Copyright © Nicky Holford 1989

Typeset in Trump Mediaeval by
The Spartan Press Ltd,
Lymington, Hants.
Printed and bound in Great Britain by
William Collins Sons & Co. Ltd, Glasgow

For my father

ONE

When they met the earth moved. He was married, she lived alone. He was famous, she unknown. His eyes showed no discretion when she was around. His hair dampened, his fingers shook. Inside he purred.

She shone as if lit by a setting sun. It was hard to hide yet she appeared calm. Inside she felt so lighthearted sometimes it was a long time after he'd gone that she could feel her steps on the pavement.

He was their only link. She resolved never to phone him. They wanted it to be exactly as it was that first time. Only one memory, only longing, no habits. But so much would happen in each day that soon deep breaths could no longer expel a desperate desire to turn a page of each other's life and read aloud.

Her answering machine became their lifeline. The first message immortalized his voice. It made her smile and laugh out loud with happiness. That he was not there did not matter. They could engineer to meet. The uncertainty of coming home perhaps to hear from him did not unsettle her. If he'd phoned it was a gift. If not, she had not missed him. Whatever he said was timeless.

It was not long before he expected to get the machine. The machine was, after all, a friend. It was the next best to her who soaked up all his thoughts. If she was not home he delighted in knowing she would come home to the tape that would have preserved his longing for her. He did not long for her to be with him but to know the dark side of his soul. Words were omnipotent to them both; they did not have to be there to speak them.

'Hello machine, heelloo machine,' he would say. In a long deep voice or a flustered, high-pitched one. He started to tell her of images that flashed across his mind and others he dwelled upon. He could lumber into an accent or two, repeat a sketch, impersonate a celebrity. As he kept talking to her on the machine a relationship developed. Gradually the familiarity of a deep friendship crystallized.

One day she could not be sure his message was for her. She was accustomed to his dark moods, his constant questioning, his unashamed playfulness. But this time she found herself wondering whether he had phoned the machine and not her. She found herself wanting to talk to him. To ease her frustration she left him coded messages, nuances only he could read, telling him when she would be there. This time he told her, he'd spoken to the machine and the machine had told him a few things.

'What?' she wondered. 'What has the machine told him?'

They met the next day. Burrowing within each other they wondered, was this perfection between a man and a woman?

He went away for his work, and the distance made her nervous. She found herself thinking about the machine, not wanting to be away, rushing home to see if he'd phoned.

He phoned every day until one day she came home and the machine seemed to mock her. The little red light that habitually flashed to say he'd phoned, was not illuminated. She flipped the controls. There was nothing, only yesterday's voice. The sadness she felt resurrected a new conflict within her. She longed not for his voice, or his stories, but for him. She fought it off, until tomorrow, she told herself.

Something was wrong. He knew the machine intimately by now. Every whirl of its spools, each scratch in the tape. For two days he felt the same.

He often started 'Is that the machine' when she spoke. But she would laugh in such an unmechanical way that he changed quickly, wiping away the stories he would have left had it been the machine. She was so pleased to hear him, he felt uneasy. She joked that the machine had them under its control. But silently he began to recognize the power of the machine.

One day she went to the phone just to hear his voice. She could dial her home number from anywhere in the world and wait for the message on the answering machine to start playing.

It normally answered on the second ring, but this time there was no answer. She tried the number again and thought back to that morning, certain she had turned the machine on. She shivered through a wave of uneasiness.

'Heeallow machine' he said. 'Do anything exciting last night, chuckle chuckle?' And with that he laughed deeply, and switched his allegiance.

He told her that last night he dreamed that he was the waves on an ocean and she came riding towards him, the pounding hooves of her galloping horse throwing the sand into his waves. She was riding naked, her long blonde hair flying like the mane of her horse in the wind. And as he reached out to her shamelessly breaking on the sand she stopped, climbed off her horse and ran into him.

'I must see you,' he said. 'Now.'

And then he sang a song he'd written for her trying to hold the telephone in the crook of his neck while he played the guitar. With a final strum and change of chord he hung up.

He felt at once that something was wrong. It is only a machine, he tried to convince himself.

When she walked through the front door she could see the flashing red light of the answering machine. It was the first time she registered his silent warning. 'I must see you,' he said and she knew that she felt the same.

They arranged to meet on a bridge where they had once had their picture taken. As he saw her waiting for him, each step seemed to take him further away. He felt the air around her long before he brushed the soft skin of her cheek. She held her head back high as she laughed, rich and full with expectation. His blushes, like an adolescent, matched his fumbling hands that longed to hold her.

At last he wanted to share the detail of his waking hours and the underworld of long nights away from her. For the first time he felt he could not live without her. They were criminals with their forbidden riches.

He said it first. He had to warn her. 'The machine,' was all he said. 'Don't let it control us.'

The next day, she woke just before dawn as he phoned. He made her tea and she heard the chink of a spoon against china as he stirred in the milk. She pictured him at home and pushed such thoughts away. She was glad that she had the capacity to turn her mind into a honeycomb of thoughts, isolating each one. If there were no compartments to shut off her feelings for him, she feared they would leak into all her thoughts.

But later when she went to leave the house she hesitated by the answering machine. She stared down at it and then turned it on.

TWO

The clouds shuffled across the sky. Rebecca watched them buff and jumble themselves into an ominous grey mass. She watched the sky often as it formed the backdrop to her thoughts. She would stand at the window, in front of the sink, washing up the few things that wouldn't go in the machine, while she tried to work out whether she was happy or not.

That word 'happy' annoyed her. But she couldn't stop herself moulding and remoulding it in her mind. It left her feeling wretched so she would slip into a mindless state keeping herself busy by perfecting the already immaculate order of her house. Not for a second did she feel that running a house, a husband and a family was demeaning. But did it make her happy?

She did not dwell on such thoughts because there was always so much to be done. The days, months and years were running into each other so quickly. Was it always like this? Were people always so busy? She thought not, remembering the time, not so long ago, when she never carried a diary. About half way through the year or if they were on sale she would buy one and try to fill it by making neat little entries. Her daughter's birthday would go in first and then Noel's. It was always Tammy first because she needed her mother and Rebecca relied upon that. Noel never needed anyone. He kept so much to himself that she had long since given up trying to penetrate that shell. She had no real idea what he thought of her. But she knew by asking no questions, by having never asked him to tell her more, she had made him reliant on her friendship.

It was 9.15 a.m., which gave her two hours to finish the ribbing on the spaceman's outfit. Thank God the new director had agreed with Kathleen that they needed something less flamboyant than the usual interpretation of space fashions. Rebecca thanked Kathleen for staying in touch over the years. It was a long time since they had been students together at the Rose Bruford Drama School with their fresh aspirations and hopes of recognition. Kathleen had thought of her immediately when her wardrobe assistant for the TV serial had walked out. Even though she hadn't worked for several years, Rebecca was grateful for the job because it had changed her routine. She would not have instigated it herself but now she realized how much having a job had restored her battered confidence.

She thought that if she smoked she'd have a cigarette now. Noel was always the smoker. Tonight they were having dinner with a couple who got under his skin. She wondered what sort of mood Noel would be in.

She took off her apron and automatically smoothed out invisible creases in her skirt. She turned back to the spaceman's outfit. She had devised a frame, not unlike a wire hanging basket onto which she was sewing a number of sausage-like shapes to make the helmet look three-dimensional. Tammy had brought home a shiny gold glue stick she had been using at school which dried into a solid spiky lump. It would give the look she wanted.

The glue refused to come off her hands. She had used too much and resorted to squeezing whole handfuls of the stuff to get the effect of spikes. She read the back of the tube which warned of dangers to the skin if the glue inadvertently wandered from its tube into contact with human flesh.

The phone rang. Noel had been held up and would be home late. He'd forgotten about dinner with the Cuthberts, and didn't like the idea. There was a silence between them. Make up your own mind, it said, but you only have one choice.

*

Tammy would be waiting by now. The school was nearby so she came home for lunch. Rebecca looked at the tiny gold spikes that covered her fingers and grabbed a raincoat. She'd only be a few minutes late.

Rebecca had tremendous poise. She usually wore her long dark hair up, but elegantly loose, not tightly pinned or fussy like the archetypal school mistress. She was tall and slim and kept her shoulders back and her long neck high. The first impression she gave was chilling. She had been called the ice maiden at school when children were too young to understand what it was to be aloof. It probably had something to do with the unfortunate knack she had of putting people on edge, making them feel as if they had done something wrong. Such an impression was far from her generous nature, but it would always take a little while to get to know her.

In the country she dealt with people on two levels. She aired her warm smile when she went shopping in the village to buy what she needed for the house. But she did not wrap words around convivial pleasantries, she minced them. Every now and then she would give Mrs Patel in the post office a snippet of gossip so she did not get left out of community affairs. Noel was the one who had charisma. He spent a lot of time in the pub and it was through him they met most of the friends who lived nearby. But she was more at home when their friends from London came up. With them her mind whipped into overdrive and the tedious details of domesticity were replaced by fun and heated debates about politics or art. On these occasions she would stretch out her thoughts, eager to pull in and digest any reaction and then move their talk forward again. Noel always said she got too serious.

When they first moved from London she was relieved to leave the smoke and noise, the people always dropping in, the constant dinner parties. She remembered so clearly waking up to the collection of glasses when she had been too tired to wash them up the night before. Overnight the last drop of claret would have congealed in the most unobtainable part of the glass, and her day would start with the stale smell of old wine.

Their move hadn't worked out the way she thought it would. Noel craved the stimulation of city dwellers to feed his mind and set him aside from his slower-paced neighbours. Not that he was ever condescending or critical of people less intelligent than himself. That was the problem. He would prop himself for hours against the bar at the pub listening in microscopic detail to the teething problems of their farming neighbour's new milking system. He would always glean something and add it to his repertoire of obscure information which would surface later. But after a few days he developed a restlessness that she knew would take him away from her.

He was in London today and she didn't know why. If she asked, he would always tell her, but she never did. She didn't want her life to change. Noel was a tight-rope walker. One slip and he would fall leaving her to clear up the mess in his wake.

Where they lived in Suffolk was hardly cut off. The train to London was a popular commuter ride to Liverpool Street. She sometimes wondered if Noel had chosen the area because the last train left quite early. She knew the nights he was going to miss it even before he'd left home.

She knew he wouldn't miss it tonight because guilt weighed heavily on his conscience. He could somehow justify himself being late – even so late that he would miss the entire dinner. But he would not miss the whole night.

Tammy was growing up fast. She was fourteen. Rebecca hated to think what the phonebill must be. Between Tammy and Noel the telephone was constantly in use. When Tammy wasn't phoning her friends, she liked to shut herself in her room and listen to music. She spent hours trying on clothes and putting on make-up. She took such trouble over her dress, playing with hair-styles and accessories that the results made Rebecca feel quite out of date. Some of her teenage friends were already so sophisticated that Rebecca felt awkward around their confident hype. Rebecca was born after the war when fashion hardly existed. But she was keenly aware of the change of emphasis from survival and necessity to pampering and luxury. The early years with Noel were already another era, she thought, and his years before she came along were further away still.

The nest of red hair which bounced on Tammy's head made her easy to spot. Noel's hair was nondescript, mostly grey now and sparse, a highly sensitive area which he tried to disassociate himself from. But even when his hair was thick and dark, there had never been even a hint of red. They used to joke about where Tammy got her colouring from.

Rebecca liked to butter bread as if she were carving paint onto a canvas with a palette-knife. First she always made sure the butter was soft because she liked to spread the whole surface, rounding the butter with experienced dexterity between the bread and the crust. Her sandwiches were works of art and her repertoire was impressive and rarely limited to the usual standbys. She made a variety of curried sandwiches, which sometimes would have five or six layers, banana, yogurt, chicken curry, sultanas and a mild curry or lime pickle paste. She made them on popadoms, nan, french bread, pitta bread or whatever she came across, with neat garnishes of fruit or vegetables to compliment the taste.

Noel loved her sandwiches, and they used to dream up wildly incompatible combinations. Some were so disgusting she could still remember the vile ingredients taking control of her tastebuds, souring her entire mouth. Once she had given Noel a lunch-box full of sandwiches. But he had taken the sandwiches out of the box, stuffed them in his pocket and forgotten about them. Weeks later he had worn the same jacket and discovered the gooey, mouldy mat of their remains. He was not a lunch-box man.

She was meeting Sophia Eccleston that afternoon. A picture of Sophia, immaculate as always, behind the wheel of her white

Jaguar drifted into her mind. Theirs was now a frigid relationship. As marriage so often changes one's loyalties, Sophia's responsibility to her husband and three children had left her no time for her friends. Sophia never had much spare time and when they met she usually seemed preoccupied.

Rebecca dropped Tammy back at school and drove through the familiar valley now coated with the summer green of sunbathed trees. Sophia usually spent the week in London leaving to the staff the upkeep of the Suffolk mansion and its acres of grounds. It was with an unspoken acceptance that Sophia would chat about the grand dinners and distinguished guests who filtered through the gates of her elegant home to which Rebecca and Noel had never been invited.

It was nothing more than coincidence that they lived nearby. Their paths had crossed occasionally on foreign ground which had made their bond at home much closer.

'I've tried to keep it to myself, to talk myself out of it,' said Sophia. 'Each time I see him, I promise to make it the last, but I can't.'

Rebecca felt Sophia's need of her confidence and gave her the reassurance in which to place her secret.

'You've slept with him, haven't you?'

The weight of such a burden, temporarily suspended, flowed through Sophia's every nerve. The years of keeping up appearances, bringing up the children, growing away from her husband, had taken an emotional toll. After all these years she was taking a risk and its excitement and danger had softened the hard lines of her face and coloured her eyes with an innocent joy.

The frailty of human nature did not leave a hint of bitterness on Rebecca, who genuinely felt sympathetic to her friend's elation and anguish. She sat and listened in the huge garden as they drank tea under the shade of a horse-chestnut tree, wondering why Sophia had chosen her as a confidante. She slipped into her own thoughts about Noel and thought it would be good for the two of them to have a holiday.

THREE

The phone rang. Not the high-pitch squeak of the new phones, but a low purr. It rang for the fourth time and he started to panic. Suddenly the chill of not being able to reach her ravaged him with desperation. For the first time he wondered what it must be like for her not to phone him. He wiped the thought away because they never thought such things.

He dialled again and willed the machine to answer. This time it worked and he mouthed the words her faraway voice spoke because he knew the message by heart. He was struggling, he told her, to put his ideas in ink. That was what he did, he poured the complexities of his thoughts onto a blank canvas until he brought it to life. When they met, he felt his thoughts pass through her. The burning fire that she lit within him kindled each stroke of his pen so that every line was alive and he longed to tell her about it. Sometimes the lines he drew would be the thin strands of her hair, a tiny vein in her leg, the ripple from a muscle in her back. He would memorize each part of her to later resurrect a fragment hidden in a drawing of something else. He worked hard and his reward in her made him all the more determined. He no longer was a struggling artist – like so many others – and that in itself set him aside, leaving him in an insular world.

Today he wanted to talk to the machine, to tell it off about yesterday's prank, which he knew was more than coincidence. So he did. And as the steam rose from his frenzy he heard a hiss like the venomous cry of a snake as the machine shut off.

He dialled the number again and it rang and rang in defiance. He looked at the canvas and fixed his mind on his work. He sucked his anger dry and stood to see it staring back at him from the shapes and colours he had painted.

She knew, naturally, that something was wrong, as she sipped cool wine and listened to the words of an admirer. Their fates were entwined and might always be. But the future would come to them and they knew enough to leave it alone.

It was her other life trying to compete with him. She had been asked away for the weekend to stay with friends where he could not phone her. There would be a change if she accepted.

When she got home that night it was late. That was when she found the broken tape. She knew he would not phone again until the morning. She pieced the tape together and rewound it to the beginning only to find there was nothing on it. That night a cold wind rippled through her and she shivered in her sleep, while all around her others threw off their blankets on the warmest night of the summer.

'Hello love, my dearest one.' He was calm, ethereal after his battle. He told her at length about his painting, the wrath that had seeped out of every pore. He knew, of course, about the broken tape but assured her it was nothing and it would work now.

He told her to go away, for it was the weekend and he could not be with her. And they fluttered and poured into each other like thick cream absolving the machine while speaking scathingly about its spools and sore heads.

She cocked her head from side to side and smiled through the large empty room where she would leave him for the weekend. She dusted the machine and gave it a new tape hoping her respect would restore its loyalty. She packed her bag and briefly entertained the thought it was for him. Then she shut the door and would have skipped down the road if her bag had not been so heavy.

*

He felt the door bang as he paced the studio and rushed to the phone. Before he picked it up he knew their line had been severed. He struggled with a terrible emptiness until he knew he was jealous. He phoned the machine to confide his turmoil and made up. 'I'm sorry,' he said and he heard the tape slacken as it turned round the spools and he knew he was forgiven.

Words that he'd never uttered before flew uncontained from his lips. He held the mouthpiece of the phone intimately, cradling it with the conflict he unravelled. He was no longer the waves on the ocean but a tiny raft that barely survived the shipwreck that left his life and his wife mangled by the pretty coral which guarded the shore.

His work was his life and she was becoming inseparable from it. That thought – which felt as if it twisted, ravaging from his heart coursing to each capillary – was a revelation. But he told the answering machine about the wearying path he took before his long warm fingers would clutch his brush and let his poetry flood or dribble onto paper.

He knew he was good. But he also knew the greatness of the true artists and only that would be good enough.

Yet he felt torn by the compromise of his life. He loved his wife and child and his house, his car, the birds that sang so piercingly each morning when he woke. Then there was her. She had cut through the padding that protected his soul as violently as a sharp knife through soft flesh and the pure blood that poured out could not be ignored. He loved and hated her for that. She had revived the impetus he needed and at the same time had brought a terror that would leave his comfortable life in shreds all around him.

So he spoke at length to the machine of his dilemma. The great warmth he felt for the people in his life that he never wanted to hurt. She was amongst those, but always different because he couldn't imagine the intensity of his passion for her dying down. He saw it on a parallel with his work, which must never be mediocre. He spoke for much longer than the length of the machine's tape but he knew the machine was still listening. When he put down the phone the room was spinning around him. Coloured canvases seemed to come towards him and then in their distortion draw back much like a hall of mirrors. He closed his eyes and ran his large rugged hand softly up her leg, round the contours of her thigh and hips, up along the crest of her back, lightly past her breast and over her shoulder scooping up along her neck like a spoon through ice cream until he turned his hand and caressed her cheek with the backs of his fingers.

FOUR

Briony Lange had long, perfectly shaped legs which she wrapped around the sofa as she lunged for the phone. When she was standing still her legs were no longer than those of any well-shaped 5′ 8″, twenty-seven-year-old. But they seemed to be continually moving. Her gestures were not sexual although the effect was sensuous. She crossed them over and over and then slithered them along the spine of the sofa.

This way she had of playing with her legs, combined with nuances she articulated through her wide dark-brown eyes, and her slightly hesitant way of speaking, immediately set her apart. She would have been striking anyway, her hair was fair and shaggy, always falling into her long dark eyelashes, traitors to her fair colouring. A thorough education had pummelled poise and confidence into every pore. But now she played with manners, with words, with her illicit freedom, to the surprise and adulation of her unsuspecting peers.

She did not fit into the mould of an Elizabeth Taylor or a Marilyn Monroe. Not simply because her legs were longer, but because her starry-eyed gaze would float far beyond the eyes of ordinary men and she was not yet primed for extraordinary men. Assuming, of course, that men were her ultimate goal. At the moment she was secure in the delicious warmth of independence, foolishly thinking herself in control of her own destiny.

From the carefully chosen chintzes which lined the french windows and covered her duvet she drifted between the sheets of a lower life. Out there on the streets, late at night, she had begun to see sights previously deleted from her precious background – the junkie shooting up with heroin, a brawl concluded with a flick knife, late night haunts, where drink and dancing left her bathed in sweat and a surreal haze.

Marcus had initiated this alternative education and she, an avid pupil, had camouflaged her fear by the hunger she had to see and learn more. During the day her fingers would slide accurately and with grace over and over the keys of her piano. The sounds of Mozart or Beethoven, Chopin or Bach would twirl around her senses while her hands worked methodically until she had to stop, her fingers aching so badly they would hang by her sides, too weak to hold a pencil. After practising all day, she was ready to let loose.

She always left the answering machine on so as to avoid any distraction that might break her concentration. It was uncanny the way Marcus phoned each time only seconds after she'd closed the piano lid. She was sure it was him phoning now.

He was a smooth-talking bastard – she loved that expression – from a suspicious background, operating in a devious business, selling packages. His gangster looks were devilishly appealing, he was shady and Briony knew he was a risk to be played with like a wild cat leaping through fire. They'd met in a lift. She on her way down, he up, the lift had hesitated over their contradictory commands. As to her specific talent, he had little interest and less knowledge. In the tiny confined space of the lift there was something unusual about Briony which aroused his curiosity. He'd crushed his card into her hand and told her to phone next Tuesday when they would meet.

Briony had not been able to resist. He had come into her mind during moments when her concentration broke. Briony already imagined him in a tall luxury building with a spectacular view. When she phoned she couldn't have been further off target. He had given her a shopping list, ingredients she would find in a Chinese supermarket and told her to buy two metres of emerald green material, as slinky as possible. Then he explained how to get to the houseboat where he lived.

When she arrived he had taken her around the narrow deck, downstairs into a room that looked like an insider dealer's depot. Computers and word processors flashed and beeped, teletext rolled overhead, telephones rang. The boat was deceptively large and the huge throbbing office could be temporarily obliterated by closing a two-inch-thick steel door, leaving an abyss of calm on the other side. Elegant beige leather sofas surrounded a triangular coffee table, while pale yellow silk curtain draped lavishly over the tiny cabin windows. The soft lighting which diffused around the room made it warm and secure.

'Please,' she remembered Marcus had said when he signalled her to sit down. It was the first word he had spoken. She looked around unable to slot the interior design into a mould, not even sure whether she felt uneasy or not.

It was a night which dipped in and out of fantasy. First they drank mango Bellinis. Then he made her a Chinese meal flipping and stirring the fresh vegetables he'd cut into bite-sized portions. Then he asked if she'd bought the material, measured her and in less than an hour cut out and sewed a dress which he made her swap with her jeans.

The night was magic and sordid. From there he took her in a smart new car to a small nightclub where they drank champagne and danced surrounded by black ties and taffeta dresses. Then he took her round the soup kitchens of the homeless where they looked pompous, patronizing, out of place dressed in finery, surrounded by the muffled tang of poverty from men and women who had not bathed for weeks. He played *chemin de fer* in Mayfair, and danced in Brixton. It was 8 o'clock when he drove her home.

They had not made love, neither that first night nor in the three months she had known him. But she had confided her only secret in him and he had one he thought of telling her.

She went to pick up the phone. It was Noel.

FIVE

Rebecca couldn't decide what to wear. She knew exactly the sort of dress Madeleine would squeeze her well-fed frame into and tried to think of the fabric she always bought, something like acrylan.

At forty-two, Rebecca had held her figure, although she never showed if off even in her youth when she was slim and lithe like a fox. As she flipped through her cupboard hoping something she'd forgotten would seem appropriate she felt sure that Noel would create a scene, if he showed up at all.

She knew his moods so well. His worries, preoccupations, the nervous pacing, the complete detachment from all that was going on about him. It always passed and she saw no difference in this particular pattern except that it had gone on for quite a long time.

The last time she wore the plain dark blue linen dress she chose was when they went on holiday to Venice. It was far too hot and Noel had developed a heat rash which he was convinced was a fatal disease. He'd insisted on seeing a doctor and became apoplectic after they'd waited in an airless basement room for over an hour. But the doctor's diagnosis reassured him, until the pharmacist gave him a prescription for constipation by mistake and he was limited to one-stop trips on the vaporetti for the rest of the holiday.

By the time she finished dressing it was 7.30 p.m. The house was blissfully quiet except for the occasional hum from passing aeroplanes. She took a sweater in case David was barbecuing, put some lipstick on and left.

They were all there sitting round the small pool, drinks in hand.

'Rebecca, how lovely to see you,' said David, who gave her a sweaty hug oblivious to the barbecue tongs hooked obscenely through his well-worn bathers. 'I'm just putting the meat on and then I'll change. What will you have to drink?'

She chose white wine and said hello to the familar faces already relaxed and glad it was the start of the weekend. 'Hello Tom, hello Meg.' They were eight, or would be when Noel arrived.

'Jerry and Morgan will be here soon,' said Madeleine as she appeared in a neat crimplene dress the same colour as her apricot slingbacks.

It was pleasant sitting by the pool with the smell of freshly mowed grass and the scent of roses in full bloom. Only one good summer's day was needed to wipe away the memories of the long, wet spring.

'Where's Noel?' Tom was the first to ask. Noel's exuberance was considered a prime ingredient and his absence was only looked upon in terms of a missing entertainment factor.

Rebecca remembered the phone call with him that morning.

'He's in town, he was worried about getting back late.'

They slid into comfortable chatter away from responsibility and warming up to fun. Tom worked in the city and Morgan had made money from ready-pasted wallpaper. Rebecca liked Morgan and looked forward to seeing him and Jerry. They were all solid characters, she thought, and reliable. They may talk about their cars and their houses and the problems with the washing machine but they would be there if she ever needed any help. She wondered if she was more like them than Noel. Morgan and Jerry arrived.

By 11 o'clock Rebecca was feeling uneasy. She couldn't believe he would miss the last train. Madeleine sat down for the first time and poured coffee. Tom was having a swim while Meg tried to throw cocktail sausages at his bare white bottom when it bobbed above the surface.

And then she heard the crackle and pop of his tyres on the gravel. He bounded in with a huge grin and a bunch of roses for Madeleine. Before Rebecca could catch his eye he took off all his clothes and with the impact of a whale flopped into the pool. Tom was the only one who didn't laugh because he'd been submerged by the ensuing tidal wave.

He was forgiven, the light in their eyes said, and Madeleine rushed to get him a plate of each and every cut of meat that had succumbed to the condensed heat of the barbecue. Rebecca didn't know what she felt except that he was further away from her than she'd ever felt before.

SIX

That night Noel's hand drifted to the far side of the bed and swept over the woman sleeping next to him. The movement blurred as the outline of another figure shaped the air under his hand. He looked around the room which was cold and dark. There was just the buzz from an alarm clock and a flutter as each minute ticked by.

He lay watching the shapes integrate with shadows, willing himself to sleep, trying to stop the night distorting his thoughts. Then he got up and went downstairs to phone the machine.

'Thank God you're in,' he said when the little peep that means 'talk now' sounded, and began to chatter nervously. His voice became steadier as he spoke and he started to walk about the room like an actor on stage until he was gesticulating extravagantly. Sometimes he would squat on the floor and sometimes he would stand as tall as he could with his hand stretched to the utmost of his reach. He talked as if he were in a confessional, or addressing a crowd at a rock concert. Sometimes his voice was soft, sometimes it boomed. What he said was really for her and he felt the machine twitch. The machine wanted to be loved, that was it, and like a jealous lover it was quite capable of not relaying his message.

He was jealous, he was writhing in jealousy of her freedom. She had never asked him anything, no demands, and that was against human nature. But he knew the sweet mutterings of her heart because he had cracked the shell and reaped the harvest of her soft contents. How he longed for her. Such longing that it gushed from him. He wanted to run his hands through her hair and hold her so close to him that he could look into the secrets in her eyes. He had never seen such eyes that led him, through a maze, into himself. That was it, he saw himself unchanged by human perception, in her eyes. Then he wondered what she felt, she who gave him new life. He must find a way to be with her, he must spend this time of the night with her. Then with her filling his thoughts he went to his studio where he painted the first in a series of paintings which would bring even greater acclaim from the critics than he'd had before.

The day had taken shape while he worked although he was oblivious to the attention the birds tried to draw. Dawn chorus in B flat, he would later tell her, pounded out a concerto while he created his own. When he finished he couldn't wait to tell her. He phoned the machine and whispered words of love, quite poetic, for a lark he said. Then he told her about the painting, their painting and that he was panting for her, which he did on the phone, sticking out his tongue and hyperventilating until the lack of oxygen made him laugh. 'Bye, love', he said and blew her a kiss that would arrive when he came to sweep her off her feet. Then he collapsed in a sofa and slept without a stir until the afternoon.

The morning light had slithered through the blinds in Briony's room and with the first sun had come her waking thoughts of Noel. Now she lay in the tall grass and thought about him again, knowing she was his catalyst. She watched her friends lying around the overgrown field as a silent film quite detached from her dream of his power over her, the sensations of his hand feeling as it did when he touched her.

Gradually it was becoming harder and harder to keep him nestling quietly in her honeycomb of thoughts as he buzzed so loudly all the way through her. Sometimes she saw herself unable to contain her longing. She would drive through the sleeting rain and dark of night to see him just for five minutes or she would break their private bond and dial the number she'd tried in vain not to memorize. Above all, she thought, he must never hear in words the feelings that drove and tormented her. She wanted only him. She knew she only wanted him if he came naturally. She vowed never to torment him with her freedom but he had no right to her when he belonged to another. Such rationale did little to quell the drive between them. This gentleness to protect each other only strengthened their fate which wrapped itself tighter and tighter around them.

In her dreams the two of them had time, minutes and hours and days to know the workings of their minds and every part of their bodies. In their soft caresses or impassioned fury they would wear each other out, obsessed with perfecting their exploration, only to find another dimple of skin that tensed to the touch or a word that made them both laugh.

In her nightmares she lived again without him. Her life so shallow without the stirring of her soul mirrored times without him. Like a cat with primed senses she knew her perfume gave off his scent. She felt she would die to hear his voice at that moment but she willed herself to wait until the evening. Then she would find a way to phone the machine.

The weekend seemed to stretch interminably in front of Rebecca. Not long ago it seemed Tammy's needs were a full-time operation, now the passing of time hit a sensitive nerve at the base of her spine.

She would start on another outfit after taking Tammy to pick strawberries. Saturday would be a quiet night, maybe she'd go to the pub with Noel. She'd make her Robert Carrier strawberry flan for Sunday when Simon Curzon, an old friend of Noel's, and his girlfriend came and then she'd talk to Noel about going on holiday.

Noel was nowhere in sight when she woke up that morning, she smiled at the unlikely picture of him going for a jog. She heard the post clatter through the letterbox and was drawn to the glistening crisp ink of an envelope whose shape distinguished it from all the other post. The Eccleston crest on the back reduced her curiosity. Its contents revealed a historic occasion, at least for her. It was Sophia's first formal offer of hospitality to them and the event was a garden party in September.

'Where's Daddy?' Tammy asked.

'I think he's working.' They both wondered as they often did, what Noel was doing. 'Ready to go and pick strawberries?' Rebecca asked, and Tammy, who was far more enthusiastic than was usual for a Saturday morning, switched her thoughts to the rows and rows of ripe fruit waiting to be plucked. She's growing up so fast, Rebecca thought. Tammy sat in the car wearing her dark sunglasses which always made her put her nose a little higher in the air.

They bumped into two of Tammy's school friends and the three girls bounded off in secrecy, the strawberries forgotten for the moment.

Rebecca started at the far end of the field, her mind filled with the Beatles' song 'Strawberry Fields Forever', which had influenced their choice of a wedding cake. Her thoughts flashed forward to December 1980, to seeing the television bulletin and the newspaper picture. John Lennon had been murdered. Noel was in New York then, and had gone to the Dakota. Lennon's death had marked the beginning of a new tough world that treated people as disposable items with no more worth than a broken toy put out of service. She remembered the hardness of Noel's face when he told her about it. Noel loved New York for many of the same reasons Lennon did. He'd lived there before he met Rebecca. She remembered him telling her that one day he was watching an ambulance force its way along 34th Street in rush hour. The pavements were crowded and the road solid with traffic. As he watched the ambulance's slow progress he knew that it would arrive too late. He had told her that was when his childhood assumption that dialling 999 would bring help, was shattered. John Lennon's death was a deeper thorn in the same wound. Tammy didn't even know who the Beatles were. Once she came home with a version of a Beatles' song jazzed up by another band. Rebecca had played her the original 'Sergeant Pepper's Lonely Hearts Club Band' and Tammy thought it was awful.

She wondered what would have happened if she hadn't asked Noel to marry her. They were driving past the Chelsea Registry office one day. She had told him she wanted to get married and have children and he had said, as he so often did, without thinking, 'yes'.

He was thinner then, with a full head of hair. She tried to remember exactly what colour it was, so dark it was nearly black. He was always the centre of attention, it seemed natural for him to perform in front of an audience and his friends grew to expect it. She felt protective towards him, content to be the one who listened while he orchestrated the crowd and smiled when asked how she put up with him.

Noel had been married before when he was twenty-one and still at art school. He fell in love with the waitress who worked in a café the students used. She was a dancer so dedicated to her work that she didn't have room for the affection Noel demanded. She was famous now. Every now and then Noel would meet her for lunch. Rebecca had met her and seen her dance, but the undercurrent of the past overwhelmed their conversation, which never flowed naturally.

SEVEN

Noel was on the phone. He was always on the phone. Rebecca knew that he used the phone when she went out. Once she had forgotten her cheque card and had phoned him for the number but the line was constantly engaged.

Sometimes she woke in the night and sensed Noel was on the phone. Who was he phoning? What was he doing?

She was beginning to hate the phone. I'm going crazy, she thought. But when the phone rang she would jolt. She wanted to confront it, stare it in the face and give it a look that could kill. Then she thought, I am stupid to hate a telephone.

But it was getting harder and harder to treat the telephone with the same detachment as the vacuum cleaner.

Occasionally she'd said, 'Who was that?' as casually as possible but Noel was quick to respond with the name of an innocent, someone who would never be a partner in crime such as adultery.

He didn't know that she knew he was on the phone. He always used the cordless phone so he could walk away. But it made a little pip which she invariably heard. It was becoming a tool of mistrust, a manipulative invention of technology, a monitor of infidelity.

At first she thought she was making it up. It was turning her life into a game of cat and mouse. She sensed that he was waiting for her to go out so he could phone, that if she stayed in he would hover, frustrated. He had even bought a phonecard. Maybe he goes out to phone, she thought. But her thoughts did not get further than the phone. The idea that there was someone on the other end of the line was dismissed by her hatred of the foul plastic beast.

It was not just that Noel spoke on the phone, he was also becoming obsessed by them. In the last three months he had bought four new phones, and for the first time put a phone jack into the studio. Until now he had never shown any interest in gadgets. He wanted to be left alone with his art, with no interruptions.

Various themes wound themselves around her mind. Noel and the telephone, Sophia and the atrocities of her infidel schemes, her work, her kitchen, her child, was she attractive? Her previously organized life was becoming muddled. There were too many variables and they were upside down and inside out at the same time.

The sun was low in the sky, its rays casting a pale hue over the hedgerows and barley stubble. Briony lay on her stomach at the end of the garden throwing blades of grass or stray leaves into the river watching them skim on the current until they wandered into the overgrown river bank.

'Come on Briony, let's go to the house and you can play for us.' Lizzie's voice jolted her back to her worries.

Sometimes she hated Noel for his hold on her. On several occasions she had nearly told Lizzie about him, but the timing was never quite right. She knew they would accept whatever made her happy, but she despaired of herself for loving him.

She could hear Greg practising and remembered how simple it was then, back at college with nothing taking precedence over their music. Ever since Lizzie and Greg married and bought the farmhouse it had become Briony's refuge. Now Noel was eating into that. It was all so natural at first until their commitment put demands on each other.

Briony could not detach herself from an obsession to find a

phone. With stubborn resolve she would not accept he hadn't phoned. She was too impatient to wait.

'No, thank you Lizzie. I really must get back,' she said, when all she meant to do was phone the machine.

Noel phoned again and left another message more desperate than the last. The house was empty, he'd told her, she could come over, what a thought. Such a suggestion catapulted through him with an excited terror of being caught out. He paced the room ready to pounce at any moment should the phone ring. He had to spend a night with her. To do so he would have to lie. Briony had wrapped herself around him and squeezed his deceit into the air. Then he wondered how he had imprisoned himself so that a single night away was a serious break in habit. He thought how, by trying to be fair, he had driven himself into a corner.

Lately, every time he went out he drove past the Dick Turpin phone booth and had to stop to phone her. They called it that because there in the middle of a field, quite alone, was a telephone. It looked like the sort of place many a highwayman would have ridden through. Phones, always phones: that was his gateway to her and now he needed her, not the grubby handpiece of a public telephone.

He had not spoken to her for two days, although the machine and he had shared many a confidence since then. He was aware of tugging loyalties, toying with the idea that she and the machine were inseparable.

EIGHT

Noel had lied bitterly. As he drove fast along the motorway he tried to unravel the knots that turned his stomach with the elasticity of a rubber band. Simultaneously he tried to curb the elation he felt. It was so wrong, cruel, weak. He tried to build up the feelings he knew were right, guilt, but it wasn't working. Each time he stepped up the acceleration his heart pounded with excitement. He would see her soon, in minutes.

Briony was not the first woman to cause him to err from the sanctity of his marriage. But he had long since settled into middle age and an accepting grace that his wilder days had passed. Sometimes he gloated in the security of his isolated life, locked with his thoughts in the country, away from temptation. There were always the two sides, the dark evil temptress willing him to live dangerously and the angel of compassion, who probably made jam.

He gripped the steering wheel and felt it shudder and tremble in his hands. A noise rose in his throat, tears welled in his eyes, anticipation filling him like the first tremors of an earthquake. He took a long deep breath and grinned, knowing it was all crazy, bad, bad craziness.

They had met at every time of day: breakfast, coffee, lunch, tea and the occasional dinner or midnight snack. But most often they would meet somewhere away from the rat race – a museum or gallery – in the afternoon. In retrospect it would always seem surreal. Even the reality of parting would have the mythical quality of a curtain shutting off the stage rather than the rubbing of shoulders in a rush hour crowd.

They had their places, a quiet restaurant, an open field, or sometimes, her flat. It was not often that they met there in the afternoon when the world was working, because it was always too hard to leave. The hours would race by. He could call up that feeling and hated it. He always wished for so much longer.

Tonight he would not have to rush. The thought of so much time swept over him, filling him with euphoria. He had not told her he had a whole night. He reined in his thoughts which were turning to her exquisite nakedness, his hand involuntarily shaping her form. He changed the tape and teased himself by thinking of something quite different.

Should she change? Into what? Or should she throw on a coat, skim her lips with gloss, or what? Noel had not given her time to think. She paced, which took her to the mirror where she saw her face changing, colour flowing into her cheeks already pushed high and taut by her smile. Her eyes mischievously widened and caught the light. She had time to pack the two champagne glasses which she had bought for him once, but he could not take them home. She relished the little things he'd given her, their memories spilling out amongst her possessions. She must take champagne although it made little difference to them. She wanted to shower him with her favourite things, but they always left each other with only a small token of their times together. It was perfect this time. So often he would take a role as her confidante, the source of her enthusiasm. She was there for him too when he was the one who doubted himself. Often her thoughts of joy would tumble down to earth with thoughts of his unavailability. But tonight, everything was perfect. Her thoughts had calmed her down, a touch, but enough to turn around the flat in a spin gathering a few things, putting on a clean blouse. Then she turned the machine on, don't collaborate without me, it seemed to say. She swore she felt its presence as she went downstairs.

At first she thought her car wouldn't start. It coughed and spluttered and burped into silence. She waited, prayed, pumped the acceleraror and turned the ignition. The engine growled awake as if from a deep sulk. It wasn't cold but damp and her car did not take favourably to this. She let the engine chug and smooth to a purr, then chose Dvorak for the ride. She wondered why Noel wanted to meet at this remote village in Hertfordshire. He never mentioned he was going there. Usually if he had an exhibition or business somewhere, he would tell her and they would plan an intricate rendezvous. But he had never said anything about this. If she was lucky she'd get there around six. Once she'd driven to Gatwick to see him for half an hour. She hoped they'd have more time than that.

Anger propelled Rebecca around the room several times until she decided, quite out of character, to snoop through his papers, drawings, and personal things.

Then she saw the numbers sprinkled on the tiny screen of the new telephone and felt short of air. Noel had bought the slick desk-top machine only the week before. It had a memory and always showed the number last dialled on its digital screen. She told herself it had to do with a gallery, or the series of drawings he was preparing for a catalogue. But her intuition told her otherwise. She found a piece of paper and hesitated before writing the number down. Impulsively she picked up the receiver and pushed the repeat button. The numbers came up as it dialled and she waited. After the fourth ring there was a click as an answering machine took over, then she heard the clear strong sound of a woman's voice. The tape must have got caught because the voice distorted and warbled giving off a noise as if it was in pain. The high-pitched beep gave way to silence. Rebecca hung up quickly, relieved that the telephone had not thrown Noel's deceit at her. There was nothing to worry about. Her sentences were not making sense. She put the piece of paper with the number on in her pocket and breathed in the fresh country air as she walked from his studio to the main house.

NINE

Noel was the first to arrive and the tumbling down pub was perfect. He'd seen the place about two years before when he'd driven from London to a gallery opening in Cambridge.

On the way he'd stopped for a drink and immediately wanted to fall into the thick cotton sheets he imagined such a place would have in the rooms which overlooked the old mill house gardens. He rang for the receptionist and listened to the click of high heels on the tiled floor as a well-groomed lady in her midforties appeared and looked at him over her glasses.

'Can I help you, Sir?'

Unlike the earlier and rare escapades during which they had ended up, late at night, in some faceless London hotel, Noel this time busied himself with detail. He saw three rooms and chose the one which overlooked the mill. It was small and spartan but blissfully comforting with its wooden frame bed, log fire and small bathroom. He ordered champagne and a bottle of mineral water. Spurred on by guilt he decided to phone the machine for a chat, but it had completely bastardised her message, somehow editing it so that it sounded as if there were kinks in the tape. He talked to it, tried to calm it down and when he hung up he felt a twinge of disloyalty.

A bath, he thought. 'I'll have a bath', but then he heard the voice of the lady with the glasses on the stairs. 'Normally at this time of the year we're completely booked. But this year even the Americans have stayed away. The ones who do come say it's the weather or the Middle East. There you are, dear, left up the stairs and right to the end of the corridor. Dinner is at eight and the kitchen closes at nine.'

She weaseled her way around the door to see Noel in a rather unusual position, leaning across the bath. 'Hello, love,' he said, and then somehow his arms were all around her.

Whenever they met they would both start talking at once. 'Did you know that . . . ?' 'I have to show you this . . .' 'I thought you wouldn't be here for an hour . . .' 'MGM liked the drawing . . .' 'The tape is super. I played it on the way here . . .'

Then they laughed, curbing and enclosing their joy when their lips met. He would get hot and small beads of sweat gathered on his wide forehead. She would laugh as she wiped them away with her cheek and he would pretend she was mocking him, 'All right, so I'm sweating,' he would say. She would protect him from misinterpretation although she knew he'd understood that she found each part of him equal in her adoration.

She flooded him with questions and he told her he had never really looked at her, too worried about the consequences. Tonight he would watch, and listen and taste and feel. 'I'll find out if you squeeze the toothpaste from the end or the middle, measure the length of your calves, the width of your tongue, the tautness of your belly.' He jumped on the bed and lunged. Her feeble struggle out from the woolly sharpness of his sweater led her to his arms. She squealed, collapsing next to him, grasping at the bedclothes for support. 'Don't do that. What will they think? I mean, oh my God! it's only six o'clock,' he said as he buried his hand in her thick hair and pulled her towards him. 'Shhh' he said. 'We mustn't make any noise, this is a respectable place, and I'm a respectable man.'

Then he sat bolt upright. 'A drink for you, Madame? Excuse me: Mademoiselle, perhaps a soupçon of champagne?'

It would take a while to relax into each other, to calm the longing that had built up since the last time they met. But it was never long before they slipped and nudged into each other.

'Noel, why are we here, in this room, quite alone?' she asked.

'Because, my dearest one, I must know if I can be without you.' Then the cork exploded with a train of bubbles cascading into the glasses she had brought. 'No, I needed you to share the champagne.' As he said this they linked arms in a traditionally sentimental embrace but they had their own layers of meaning to make such a gesture fitting. 'Now what do you mean, you can't play what's his name's concerto?'

'Rachmaninov. The last movement of No. 2. I don't know quite why, but I can't seem to translate the music from my head through myself, my hands, onto the keyboard. It's such a wonderful piece of music but I can't seem to interpret it. I don't know, maybe I haven't played it enough. Last night I couldn't sleep. I turned the radio on and Vladimir Ashkenazy was playing that same movement and I knew he was playing it the way it should be played.'

'Did you tape it?'

She shook her head. 'No, I wanted to practise more and then let you hear me play it. Do you know what I mean? When you know you can do something. You feel it, yet it's not quite there, somehow it hasn't clicked.'

Noel nodded in agreement and smiled. 'Yes, I know. Sometimes I have a drawing in my mind which is quite different when it gets on paper. Sometimes what is on the paper is better. Sometimes what is in my mind is only the beginning, a vague form of what later takes shape as I work. And sometimes I have a picture that I can't get down on paper. But that's the artist in you and the artist in me. You have to keep trying over and over again. You know what I said about leaving it for a day or two and then going back to it? Leave it now.'

They would switch constantly from trivia to what they both called 'their work'. Oh God! he loved to hear her talk about her music and she took such comfort in what she referred to as learning from his experience. But if she ever implied that he was more experienced he would say:

'That's right, I'm too old for you. I'm no good. You'll have to find yourself another bloke, one of these young layabouts with lots of money!'

They planned their evening with such enthusiasm that in their eyes the toughest piece of beef would taste like fillet and the meanest wine would seem vintage.

'What shall we do with all this time?' he said as he slipped his warm hand down the back of her neck where he could just reach a tiny spot which sent a shiver down her spine. Sometimes if she was nervous, he could play her flesh and feel it respond. Tonight she was relaxed and he could almost feel her skin reach up to his hand begging for more like a cat in full purr. 'Shall we?' he said.

'Oh! I don't know. It's not even dark yet, this is obscene!'

'Well, I'll just take off my shoes.'

'So will I.' But she took off his shoes and burst out laughing.

'What's wrong? It's my socks. You don't like my socks? I got them in America, you know, from a famous actor who once lent them to Bob Dylan, so they must be all right. What do you mean you don't like them?'

'They are very nice,' she said.

'Nice, what sort of word is that? Nice is the most ordinary word meaning nothing, they're not nice, they are original.'

'Well at least they match your shoes.'

'So you don't like my shoes either?'

'No, I didn't say that.'

'Then why are you laughing, it's my shoes, isn't it, not my socks?'

'Why don't you take your trousers off?'

'Now it's my trousers, you want me to take them off so you can laugh at something else. No, I'm going home, you're trying to seduce me. You're using your womanly wiles. I'm just an ordinary man, an honest man with human compassion, minding my own business and here I am suddenly caught by your spell. It's too much, I'm too old for this.'

Then he made for the champagne, suddenly pouncing on her for the split second she was caught by surprise. But wrestling with her was no fun because she wasn't resisting, so he tried animal magnetism instead. This time she responded. When he could feel the hot air of her breath and the increased rhythm of her heartbeat he pinned her down holding both arms so she couldn't move.

'What's wrong with my socks.'

But she was laughing far too hard to satisfy him with a reply.

After they made love he sprang up from the tousled bedclothes. 'Look at this,' he said. 'What will people think? I'm going to draw a bath.'

'And I think I'll have one,' she said winking.

'What do you call that?'

'A wink.'

'But you closed both your eyes.'

'Well, I'm not very good at winking.'

'What about raising your eyebrows, individually of course? Can you do that? Look.'

'No, I can't move my face very well.'

'What about this, look at this one.' He was contorting his face into weird, terrifying expressions, the vampire look, the translucent terrorface. He was very good.

'I'll teach you to wink' he said, showing off his repertoire. 'In the bath.'

TEN

When Noel announced quite unexpectedly that he was going to London and would have to spend the night there, Rebecca was too stunned to react. In retrospect it was a perfectly logical conversation. She knew Noel had a meeting at the Royal Academy at 4.00 p.m. She also knew that he had a dental appointment the following day.

As he told her, she found herself fiddling with a small piece of paper in her pocket, it was the paper with the phone number she had taken from his studio.

She was meeting Sophia for lunch that day. By the time she got back Noel would have left. She knew her husband sensed her tension but he obviously decided to let it pass.

Her first reaction was to go to the bedroom and sit at her small dressing table. She started to put on make-up, which she rarely wore, and curled her long thick black hair. The image that stared back from the mirror was listless but improved when she opened her eyes wide and smiled. She changed into a white knee-length skirt which emphasized the curve of her hips and put on a pair of low-heeled sandals. It really was time Noel repainted the bedroom, the ruddy brick-red paint had started to flake and it was much too dark a colour anyway. She thought about her work and made a mental note to buy more cotton on the way home. She was behind with her sewing and could spend the evening finishing the sequinned bodices.

When she was ready she went out to the studio to say goodbye to Noel. He was bent over a drawing she hadn't seen before. 'Hello, love, what do you think?'

'It's the poster for Greenpeace.' He had drawn a huge boat equipped to cull seals. Its bow was the jagged jaws of a shark and its prey a small vessel of Greenpeace supporters.

'It's good. Noel, I have to go now.'

'All right then, I'll see you tomorrow – you better not send my love to Sophia,' was all he said.

As she turned to leave she noticed that there was no number on the telephone screen.

Unusually for her, Sophia was early. She waved gaily to Rebecca, who slipped into the booth opposite her. The restaurant was too pretentious for the clientèle it attracted, but Rebecca always enjoyed the charade the waiters played treating the dining experience as if it were a three star french restaurant in the wine country. But this was Bury St Edmunds, close enough to the train tracks to hear an occasional whistle over the piped music.

Her friend had undergone a transformation. She bubbled and chattered like a schoolgirl, her skin was smooth and rosy, she'd lost weight, and was anxious to please.

'What would you like to drink?'

'Campari,' said Rebecca. Sophia was already twiddling her cocktail stick in a double-measure gin and tonic.

'How's tricks?'

'I'm sorry?' Rebecca hadn't understood.

'Tricks. It means "things", a general sort of "how's it going" expression. That's what David said.'

Oh dear, thought Rebecca, it's still going strong. 'Is he American, your David?'

'His mother is, from New England, one of the old money families, but his father is a Scot.'

'You must be careful, Sophia. What if Darwin ever found out?'

'He can't. He's married as well you know – David. Yesterday we met for lunch. He told his wife he was going to the dentist, I felt so dishonest.'

Rebecca swallowed the sudden lump in her throat.

'How's Noel?' Sophia tried to ease the silence.

'Oh! He's fine.'

'You mean growing up?'

Sophia and Noel took no great comfort in each other's company.

'Come on Sophia, you know you and Noel will never get on, I don't tease you about Darwin or David.'

'I should phone the answering machine,' said Briony. They had bathed together, shared a few jokes and were ready for a drink before dinner.

'It's not working.'

'How can it not be working?'

'I tried before you got here. I think it feels left out if we are together.'

'That's ridiculous, it's only a machine.' The words were out sooner than she knew she didn't mean them.

'That's not what you really think, is it?'

'No.'

'Perhaps you better try.'

Noel went to the bar while she dialled the machine. 'Hello,' it said, 'this is Briony . . .' The message was fine. There was a message for Marcus which could wait and a hang-up. She went to brush the tangles out of her hair and joined Noel in the bar.

What to drink after champagne? That was Noel's first decision and he liked the ease of it – more champagne, but then he thought a beer would go down well and a nice – no not nice, he smiled to himself – special bottle of wine with dinner.

He didn't like her phoning the machine. It made him feel jealous. He laughed at his own foolishness. But he didn't like the idea that he confided in the machine and it was in control. He had told that scumbag piece of electronic technology things that he hadn't told his own wife, and suddenly, he felt a pang of guilt as he thought of Rebecca alone at home.

Why did the machine sound so warbled before? He had felt sure that it was protecting them from something or someone. Why did he have these intuitive feelings about that machine?'

A few heads turned when Briony came into the bar wearing a sleeveless top and pair of turned-up culottes which showed off her legs. Noel watched. He shivered with the whirlwind of feeling inside him – it was certainly lust. The idea of suppressing such raw desire was quite fun. God, she was lovely. God, he was using the word God all the time.

He stood up as she approached. 'What would you like to drink?'

'It's fine, the message is absolutely fine.'

'But it can't be. I phoned it before you got here and it wasn't working. I could hardly recognize your voice.'

'There was a hang-up,' she said. 'There wasn't a message from you.'

'I didn't hang up.' They both felt someone was spying on them. 'No one ever hangs up,' she said, 'without a reason.'

Such an idea, that someone was watching them, maybe knew their secret only refreshed a thought that lurked continually in the back of both their minds. They could love each other tonight, but not tomorrow.

'A glass of dry white wine please,' she said to the approaching bartender.

Noel liked an audience, and a few lone drinkers in a country pub were perfect. He was proud to be with Briony and it didn't take long for him to strike up a conversation with one of the locals.

The man's name was Ben who out of politeness asked Noel what he did. They were near Constable's land, Ben told them when Noel said he was an artist. Noel thought he insinuated that Constable was a better painter than he would ever be. 'You're taking it too personally,' said Briony. Noel had got Ben's back up.

'Well it is personal,' he said. Briony had told him to calm down, when Ben went off to join his friends leaving tension in the atmosphere.

The dining room was inviting with a large open fire blazing in the hearth. Briony couldn't feel her feet as she glided, in a daze, to her seat. Noel, Noel, I love you, she thought to herself, letting words romance her. If only we could keep this moment. The waiter seated her, and as he unfolded her napkin she hid her wishes behind the menu. When she felt composed again she dared to look at him and saw that he felt the same.

'What is love?' he said. 'Whatever it is I don't believe in it. A word that's so loosely bound, it can certainly mean nothing which is universal. If I am fated to spend the rest of my life with you, then I'll do it for whatever the reason is, but it won't be love the way either you or I have grown to know it.'

So he had said for the first time aloud, an inkling of a thought, a tiny straw for her to grasp onto, because even as she denied it to herself she longed for their future. But what woman in love with a married man would ever dare to admit such a thought, dream or manipulation?

The need to order their food allowed them to turn away from such intense thoughts.

'I bet you'll have lamb. Yes, the crown of roast lamb with spinach,' she said.

'I don't like spinach. I'll have french beans with lamb. And, I think you'll choose something delicate like the lemon sole or maybe meat, a good hunk of beef. Yes, I think you'll have steak – and that way we can have red wine.'

'You're not guessing at all, you want red wine! I'll have the steak!'

The etiquette of ordering, of sitting politely, at their table, although she had taken off her shoes to wedge her stockinged feet up his trousers, was perfectly in contrast to the wild abandon they nurtured for each other.

'If this table was a piano I know I would be able to play Rachmaninov or any piece of music ever composed,' she said, as she played a sonata to her bread and butter.

'After dinner, I shall make love to every part of you. Kiss, and bite and lick until I have completely taken you over.'

'I don't even know how you sleep. We have never had a night and a morning. I hope you don't snore. But then again with all that licking perhaps you're not a man at all but a werewolf and tonight I'm sure there's a full moon!'

She could never remember a meal that passed so quickly. She blamed the service but it wasn't that, they had so much to say, each cutting the other off, each immersed in the other's stories. She even had cheese, which she left, in an attempt to make their precious time longer. 'But we have the whole night,' he said, aware of the hours that had already slipped by.

As they sat in front of the fire that blazed in the sitting room they were the only ones still up. The moment was much the same as the first time they had met nearly a year ago. When their bodies had seemed transparent, just a shell, as they saw straight into each other's hearts.

He slid his hand on top of hers and looked into her eyes with such penetration she fought not to look away. Her eyes matched his, self-conscious, until they crossed an invisible line of shyness. They stayed like that in silence. Then with his eyes firmly on hers, he raised his hands up to the sides of her face and brought her mouth to his.

He broke off suddenly. 'Come on, my love. Let's go to bed.'

The dying embers had warmed the room leaving the frost to

claw the windows, trying to penetrate the rich woody smell. Noel peeled Briony's clothes, feeling the heat filter through as they fell like skin from a ripe peach.

His embrace brought her down in a spiral to the carpet in front of the fire, where at his leisure he rolled slowly over her. From there he unfastened her stocking, unwrapping her as he would a fragile gift. He made sure his fingers touched each part of her leg, squeezing flesh through his fingers, stroking the thread of her muscles. Then he began to massage and knead softly, making sure not to neglect even the skin between her toes, the ball of her foot, the arching of her foot in response.

At length his tongue caressed each toe, as if tracing mountain peaks. The other leg received the same exquisite pampering, when it would twitch from time to time with delight. Her perfect legs were naturally supple and from where she lay, Briony could stretch the leg already rewarded until it reached the firm muscles in Noel's back as he leaned over her. With her toes she worked his back, nudging in between his shoulder blades down his spine until his belt cut off her access. The more she tried to wedge her foot down the tighter his belt seemed to grip. This only made her want him more. But he would have none of it. He would make her wait.

Only when she was completely naked did he let her help him with his clothes guiding her hands until they reached the green fluorescent tartan of his acrylic socks.

'Don't say I will even grow to like these.' But his lips were again on hers. He circled her mouth, the contours of her nose and high cheekbones, kissing her eyes, playing her eyelashes with his tongue and boring into the fine nerves around her ears.

With her first gentle moan he pulled away to look at her, to kiss her full on the mouth, as if to say 'I'll be back'. With the tip of his tongue, barely touching, he copied the line of her body, letting her contours choose his path as he passed her breasts, the undulation of her birdcage ribs, her soft mossy belly, the taut skin across her hip bone down the outside of her thigh to her calf, her ankle, her tiptoes. He traced her outline as if she were the chalked image of a cut out, teasing as he sensed her blushes, playing with smooth languid continuity. His longing to deviate from his route into the secret garden he would soon possess was driving him wilder and wilder into her beauty, into a dizziness, where they were fugitives.

He forced himself briefly into this world, back to her ankle, so fine he could ring it with his hand, up her calf to the soft warmth of her thigh and the source of her heat where she shivered in response.

'Noel,' her breath formed his name. Her appetite was wet. Now it was as if each capillary, each cell, every surface of her skin was crying out for his touch. If his tongue was thundering down her spine her thigh would beg for attention. If he kissed and sucked her nipple she awaited his tongue's downward journey. She was stretching, reaching and reaching, and tensing, writhing to the rhythm of his touch, and excitement.

He set out to run his lips over every surface, dragging his tongue over her white shoulders, her breasts and her powderpuff stomach in which he rested his head breathing in its scent. He inhaled her firm honey skin, burrowing his way to the warmth of her thighs, where he stayed.

She wanted him so badly she felt she would die without the feel of him inside her, clinging to her impatient flesh. She would rise up, arching her back in a rainbow, to offer her treasure. Her head was light, her equilibrium disturbed, she had only dreamed of feeling like this before.

She was blessed with a beautiful shape. Not skinny like a boy or buxom like a Ruben's model, but a combination where her skin lay smooth around her magnificent boneframe. Her hands and feet were long and slender and her stomach soft as chamois leather hung tight between her hips. The outline of her ribs rippled up to her firm rounded breasts where her nipples danced. To Noel it felt as if he had a waterfall of diamonds in his hands, as if the brightness and heat of melting gold was flowing through his veins.

'Look at me,' he said. And as he rolled himself on top of her their eyes met in silent moans. Then he kissed her, their lips brushing together like silk, then oozing stronger like warm butter until the force of his lust swept over him.

It was well into the evening before Rebecca had any time to herself. That night was no exception. A neighbour had dropped round for a chat. She'd made jam from the left-over fruit, and then a crumble for dinner. Tammy did her homework and the two of them had made a lamb casserole.

By the time Tammy had settled to watch television and Rebecca washed the last few saucepans it was past nine o'clock. She was tired by the time she started to measure up and line the first of the seven costumes. Neatly she pinned the ribbons of sequins onto the bodice and found a matching cotton.

It was quiet in the house and she barely missed Noel's presence. Most evenings he was there, playing the guitar, loafing around the sofa, restless as always unless he was reading a book or reacting to a newspaper article. Often he would work late into the night, after he had eaten and rustled up a few entertaining stories at dinner. Sometimes he'd go to the pub, only occasionally would he watch the television. He never relaxed much and Rebecca often found him tiring to be with. There were times she found the way he managed to look at everything as if it was for the first time refreshing, other times she found him childish.

She wondered if Tammy had sensed any uneasiness between them. Children were intuitive, always more clued up than they let on. Tammy was bright and had inherited Noel's imagination. It was amusing to see some of his mannerisms toned down in her. Tammy hadn't thought twice about his absence. But she had been on the phone for most of the evening. It was sweet, the way she and Noel talked, Rebecca thought. He'd always make a point not to pressure her into feeling she should be creative. 'Just tell them it's a job,' he always told her when her friends asked about him.

Occasionally newspapers rang up for quotes or interviews and sometimes a television crew would film him. Since they lived near the TV studios he joked that they only wanted to interview him when there wasn't anything else happening that day.

Everything was undisturbed. The smell of the evening meal still wafted through from the kitchen, the hot wood from the fire warmed the room. It was a huge room with a wooden floor, the fire glowing within its imposing stone mantelpiece. Rugs they'd brought back from the Middle East and other travels lined the floor with their woven stories of earlier centuries. The stereo, an expensive one, blew the last movement of a clarinet concerto around the room.

All was as it was most nights of the week, except that Noel wasn't there and except for the tiny piece of paper which kept finding its way to the tips of her fingers.

It wasn't the consequences that led her to phone but a sort of masochistic curiosity, a feeling that knowing the truth was a kind of justice that would be fairer than trying not to uncover Noel's lies. If, of course, he was lying. They had never talked about the wall that had suddenly sprung up between them. For all his faults, hurting other people's feelings was not one of them. This more than anything else weighted her suspicions.

She waited until she was quite alone. She didn't worry about the time of night, perhaps because she didn't expect an answer. Then she dialled the number, a London number, and listened to the ring.

ELEVEN

Before years of early mornings, nappies and domestic details had consumed most of Rebecca's waking hours, her nature was that of an academic. Unlike the majority of her classmates an hourly lecture analysing the finest points of Jane Austen, the inconsistencies of T. S. Eliot's work or the language of Chaucer, absorbed her concentration.

She had turned her literary talent to languages. First she studied French at the Sorbonne and later she went to the University of Padua. Quickly she grasped the nature of verbs and sentence construction of the Italian written language, but the amorous intentions of its natives, the raw uncontained and completely undisciplined lashings of emotion that appeared inseparable from everything else, made her ill at ease. Her sensibilities were curtailed to orderly perfection not spontaneity, a curious fascination with objects rather than emotion. Italians, for her, went against the grain. So she returned to France where she studied the works of Flaubert, Stendhal, Molière and Beaumarchais, the qualities of life such as fine wines and food, clothes, flower arranging and sewing.

Her natural poise became embellished with the trappings of high breeding. It was not long before she found herself on a circuit whose agenda consisted of frequent poetry readings, concerts and theatre. It was at one of these events, *Cyrano de Bergerac*, to be precise, where she fell in love.

Her affections became centred on a charismatic and extremely handsome Frenchman by the name of Jean-Louis de

Marchais. Under his influence she became quite reckless. She took in her stride the sudden change from her meticulous study to frivolity. Whereas she previously abstained from alcohol she would share not one but two bottles of champagne with Jean-Louis, or Lou as she affectionately called him. With Lou on the scene her top marks took a rapid fall as did the respect she had earned from her teachers. Her pale skin became coloured by the bags under her eyes from too many late nights and lack of sleep. The sharpness of her mind dulled until she determined to come to grips with herself. Shortly after she resolved to change her errant ways Lou invited her to the South of France for the summer and then she knew how serious he was about her.

If she drifted back in thought to that summer she could smell the sweetness in the air from the blossoms of mimosa, the poignant, aromatic scent of the trees and herbs that baked in the provençal sunshine. She was sure she had encapsulated the memory of Lou perfectly. He would be diving off the yacht, his tanned figure disappearing into the dark turquoise waters. He called to her and she would follow. She was not a strong swimmer but he had been patient with her building up her confidence. They would swim to a rocky cove, isolated from mankind where he always found a tiny beach of white sand, a cave or a bed of soft pine needles. The sun would dry them quickly leaving fine lines of salty crystals from the Mediterranean that they would taste on their tongues as they kissed. There succumbing to the magnetic influence of nature they would make love. On their return to the boat they would satiate the appetite they had worked up – either by a picnic or they would sail to one of the coastal restaurants and join the lunchtime crowd already immersed in shellfish or the local bouillabaisse. Then the siesta, the evening, the dresses, the dances, the barbecues. But Rebecca could not tease her thoughts any further, it was too painful.

Her mind did not focus on warmer thoughts. Instead it choked her back to the phone call. All she had succeeded in doing was doubling her doubt, feeding her imagination with a snippet, which, if dwelled upon, would soar out of proportion. The girl's voice was mesmerizing, cheerful, naive, fresh, but she was out. So was Noel. Rebecca had successfully justified this obscure coincidence by will power. But who was she and how could she find that out from Noel? If she didn't find out she knew it would niggle, the answering machine, the voice, the girl's or young woman's voice. It was definitely a young woman. A tall young woman with fair hair she thought.

She looked at her watch. Noel would be at the dentist, she thought, if he was going to the dentist. No she would not check, it was too desperate.

He woke up drowning in her skin, flooded by her scent. He dared not move because he wanted to watch her sleep. She was now an integral part of his arm cushioned in the folds of his skin that rearranged for her comfort each time she moved. Her lips, slightly open had fallen asleep in his, but sleep had later prised them apart. He wished to frame her head with his hands, resting her lips on his. Their faces so close their breath inhaled each other's air. He lay to savour the hazy moment willing time to dispel for ever its sense of purpose.

She moved into him, closer, so their noses touched, their breath caught in a tunnel of cheek. She lay partly on her side her legs in between his, an arm draped over his shoulder. He felt her sucking at his warmth, burrowing deep. She stirred, her eyes slowly taking him in. They closed again, hypnotized by the weight of sleep. But he could not keep from touching her, his hands as cautious as a thief, precise, intuitive, so that when she stirred he was already inside her.

She could not be sure if she was dreaming as she tried to identify and separate the thoughts and feelings that swivelled inextricably within her. She had awoken with him inside but he went so deep it was not easy to pull the dream away. His weight drew her closer, his moment was near. Suddenly he was branching out inside her, spreading tributaries, pouring his sense through her. His power made her dizzy, floating between the physical proof of her presence and the joining of their souls. He shrank back, holding her to him as if trying to hold onto every part of her at once, until sleep entangled them both.

The breaking of day did not end their night. The ebbing of time did nothing to diminish their tighter bond. No staleness or cold dose of reality could break their ties of closeness. They took strength and pleasure in everyday habits. The day would offer something new although it would also take them apart.

When it was finally time to throw back the covers they thought it fair instead of wishing for more, because that would seem too greedy. Now she could find out what jam he liked, on toast, and he would watch her brush her hair noticing that it was matted with tangles.

Briony turned on a small tape recorder she had brought with her as she waited for the bath to fill. There was news, there was life. Even in the quietness of the waking garden she heard the screech of car tyres, the hooting of horns in the distance, the hum of traffic. Her own humming camouflaged such thoughts. Echoing around the walls she left peals of squeals as she set upon tormenting her unsuspecting lover.

Noel in water had been compared to a whale too many times for his imagination to stick by illusionary masculine firmness. Packed between the bath's small borders he was definitely beached. Defenceless, he wallowed within his porcelain confines resisting her advances feebly and leaving a terrible mess. He dried himself vigorously, flexing his muscles, pruning his chest and then he caught her, squeezing his toothpaste from the middle of the tube.

Later they closed the door on a room bathed in appreciation. Sheets rumpled from wandering lust instead of sleepless nights, a nearly empty champagne bottle, a kink in the carpet. With them they took their glows, his from the rushed blood of love-making hers the burning cheeks from unshaven kisses.

The dining room was now austere and hushed conversation filled the morning.

When they had spread the tidy lace napkins on their laps and strawberry jam on their toast they started to make plans.

'I have to be in town tomorrow.'

'I have a lesson at four o'clock.'

That was their plan. They both knew the answering machine would execute it, fix the meeting place and the time.

'Let's go for a walk before we leave,' which they did, hand in hand, memorizing the colour of the sky, the smell of the air and its flavours of pine, leaf and flowering heather.

Their parting was brief, although a little desperate. Consolation lay in knowing this time it would not be for long. They started their engines and drove in unison until their separate roads divided them.

Noel had an image in his head which he wanted to get down on paper. It had nothing to do with Briony but it was a complex meshing of colour taking the form of a landscape around a face. It was a face he knew but couldn't match the features flashing in and out of mind. Each time he caught one it slipped out again. The place, that was familiar too, but he couldn't remember it. He let the colours and the image float for a while and then tried to get them into a shape.

He was a gentle man although his features portrayed confrontation. Perhaps it was the roundness of his cheeks or the inquisitive penetration of his deepset, brown eyes. His physique implied bounce rather than bulk. He was feeling good, which, since he had come closer to the milestone of fifty, was not a daily occurrence. Fifty was now less than a year away and he didn't like the idea of being on the other side of it. So far he had escaped close clashings with death, but he had seen it around him in his friends. He was at an age when clinging to life became a conscious undertaking. The other side of fifty, he didn't like the idea at all.

His appeal was not physical although his eyes hinted at attractive complexities beneath the surface. His mind was constantly alert, he was always ready for a risk or challenge, a desire for knowledge which led him into bizarre and exhilarating situations. An audience would naturally gather around him, towards his spark and vivacity which others fed off. His stories and jokes were often too far-fetched but he made them credible. Alone he worried, to the extent of paranoia, but this raw, tense energy primed him and fuelled his work.

Briony made him feel young and supple, even lithe, he smiled at such an image. The way she wrapped herself around him, undemanding affection. He clenched the steering wheel and started to sing, imitating the boom of a baritone. The paints he needed were out of the cupboard, lining up for his brushes. He knew his work would be good today.

Looking around the studio, surrounded by his work, he knew it was still a conscious undertaking to stick by his convictions. Despite an impressive number of exhibitions and publications of his work the commissions that came his way were rarely what he wanted to do. He intended to mount a show of his own but loathed the commercial gallery set-up and he was not consistently academic, at least not enough to be asked to show at the Royal Academy. He kept in touch with the people who had influenced him while he was there as a student and a teacher. One day, when he was dead perhaps his work would get the recognition he knew it deserved. Each time he gave a painting away he always wondered if its market price would go up once he wasn't around to paint another.

Rebecca was not home. Then he remembered, she had gone to town to deliver some of the costumes. She had wanted to coordinate their meetings so they could come home together. Noel made a coffee and looked around the kitchen feeling like an intruder. He thought Briony would be practising now. He liked to think of her poring over the keyboard while he flicked paint onto a brush. Often he felt lonely squeezing that intangible force out of himself, whatever it was, that made him draw. It was an incentive to think that someone out there was doing the same. He got encouragement from her discipline and determination. If she lapsed, it was never at the same time as he, so they goaded each other on.

He took his coffee to the studio, breathing in the fresh dampness, watching the steam from his mug distort in the air. But when he got there, the distractions stopped. The shapes from his head were still undefined. As they touched the paper they started to take form. He went over and over the lines, clinging to a clue, playing with another until bit by bit it started to flow. Then he would lose it only to retrieve it again stronger and more articulate. And so he worked for many hours building from nothing what he knew would become something.

By the time he was ready for a break it was already dark. He wandered back to the house realizing how unusual it was for there to be no one home. Although he had bought the house, it wasn't his at all. Others had made their lives in it and he was a casual observer, dropping in for tea.

It was a large old house with seven bedrooms, or rooms which could be turned into bedrooms. He'd given up trying to keep the damp at bay and from time to time would simply repaint bubbling crevasses that erupted and shattered his last matt finish. The ivy which mountaineered the north front was more persistent than the leafy covering that first endeared him to the place when he bought it nine years ago. The upkeep was crippling, but that was the price for an 18th century manor with old charm and no mod cons. Rebecca had decorated most of the rooms, except for their bedroom and the living room. Noel preferred a spartan look, bare floorboards, oriental rugs, no ruched curtains and no flowers. Rebecca's taste was more refined, so to compromise they each had their own dressing room. In the bedroom thick cream curtains with a simple ribbon of colour on the pelmet complimented warm, brick red walls and solid oak furniture.

Noel warmed his hands on the Aga, as a matter of habit and stoked the coal. He heard the gravel spit and saw a car draw up.

'Thanks for the lift.'

'Hiya Dad. Did you have any fillings?'

Noel jolted into a low gear, somehow the clutch stuck. Lying to his daughter chewed his stomach.

'Hello, love. No, all's fine. How was school?' Grateful to change the subject. Schooltalk must have been invented for parents he thought, as he ruffled Tammy's shock of red hair.

'It's OK. What were GCEs like? Did you do them Dad?'

'Well, yes, they were exams, you weren't assessed on your school work, you would have mock exams with similar questions but it was the exam results that counted.'

'Yuck! I'd hate that. What happened if you failed?'

'You just had to take them again until you passed.'

'Did you fail any?' She looked concerned.

'Yes, I failed maths twice,' he smiled at the memory. 'And after the first time I wasn't allowed out until I'd passed. I had to sit at home doing equations all night long. Everyone gave up when I failed the second time. Do you know when Rebecca will be home?'

'No, but Mummy said I could go over to Jen's after my homework.'

'I'll walk you over when you've finished,' Noel felt like a walk and it was on the way to the pub.

Tammy had clattered away, climbing the stairs two at a time, with her satchel and red hair bouncing in syncopation.

'I'll give Briony a ring,' he thought, forgetting about the machine which, of course, was the one who answered.

TWELVE

Briony was tormenting herself. Wielding a knife in a fresh wound. She was listening to Vladimir Ashkenazy playing Rachmaninov. Her piano teacher said it had something to do with her not being Russian, her inability to translate the soul of the piece. But she had slavonic connections she argued, her grandfather was Latvian. What about Mozart, Ashkenazy could play that as well, and he wasn't Viennese. And what about all the Japanese pianists who gave concerts?

'Your emotion is too naive,' was the criticism from Natalie Silvie. Her composure infuriated Briony, making her feel like a gangly schoolchild, arms and legs and wild ideas flapping about with no direction. She had to harness herself, discipline her feelings, channel and filter them through logic to formulate a more balanced equation.

Noel had unsettled her. Their time together had been too perfect. She was already savouring isolated incidents so she could drink reminiscences. She felt the strain that one minute he possessed her, and now she was back in her life and the change was too sudden. She would make the transition only to hear the telephone ring, and it would be him. Even if they talked about something quite mundane, gardening, his clothes, her nose which he teased her about because it had a small ridge which he called a ski jump, she had to absolve herself of him before she could get on with her things again.

She resolved, as she did each time she saw him, to stop him

going so deep, to treat him as Natalie would have her play the piano, with feeling and control.

He was probably in his studio now, she thought, motivated by his devotion. She would play for three hours before her lesson. Hard work would justify her seeing him again so soon. She locked him away and lifted the piano lid.

Briony had no great ambition but a standard she aspired to. Music had always been the quiddity around which her life revolved. She had a few regular engagements, a small bar in Soho, the tea room at the Godsbury Hotel. Once a month she joined the Main Street Cavaliers at Marengo's where she played an electronic keyboard, her only deviation from the classics. Natalie opposed it but grew to moderate her fears of a jazz influence and once even came to a jam session.

Briony's first instrument had been the flute. She had been accepted at the Royal College of Music as a flautist, but later changed to the piano. She'd met Natalie through one of her teachers. Natalie only took on new students occasionally which had made Briony far more nervous when auditioning before her, than at her end of college exams.

Briony idolized Natalie, the way her perfect, spidery fingers touched and danced along the keys. She had trained under Messiaen, which awed Briony even further.

Natalie was preparing her for a series of minor concerts and recitals anxious that Briony should learn to play for an audience. Lately she had noticed Briony's concentration fluctuating uncharacteristically. She was convinced an audience, even quite a small one would add another dimension, reappraise the mental framework behind her music. Briony was different to most of her students. There was a constant restlessness about her, a hunger she wasn't sure what for. Her discipline needed rewarding.

Briony took a deep sigh and adjusted the piano stool. It was already at the right height, because she was the only one ever to sit at it, but to raise it and then lower it to exactly the same position was more of a mental preparation to steady her composure. She turned to Rachmaninov. She would not give up on this piece.

When she finished, she had the satisfaction of knowing it was the best she had ever played it. Time had galloped by as always but she was never late for her lessons, even if, as today, a taxi was the only way of getting there in time.

Noel had just finished with the machine when Rebecca came home. They stared at each other like strangers and spluttered into conversation. She wore her suspicions like a mask which Noel saw as she side-stepped around him to hang up her coat.

He crumpled inside as guilt pierced his conscience and said something foolish. Words fell out and he heard them as a recoil. 'Would you like a drink, love? Look, why don't we go out for a bite? Tammy's going over to Jenny's and I bet you don't feel like cooking.' They never went out on their own and he sensed Rebecca sizing up this break in habit.

'Yes, all right, we could try that new restaurant off the High Street. I'll clear up in the studio.' He almost ran but his legs wouldn't carry him, deserting in the line of battle he thought. He checked his pockets for the notes she often wrote, searched his clothes for fair hairs, looked at the phone in case it would somehow give him away. He saw Rebecca's pained look, the momentary flurry of a smile cloaked by caution. He stretched and clenched his hands, did a huge o-shape with his mouth until the skin pulled. When he saw her again he'd convinced himself back into her life.

'I think we should have a holiday,' said Rebecca. 'We didn't go away this summer. Just you and I. It's been years since we went away, you and I.'

'Yes, why not?' He wasn't paying attention.

That's exactly what he said when I suggested we got married, Rebecca thought.

They were in the finishing throes of a laboured meal. The

silences between the waitress's attentions had hung in the air, dispersed occasionally by common ground, fixing the boiler, getting *The Independent* delivered.

'Is there anywhere you would like to go?'

'No love, I'm sure you have somewhere in mind.'

'Italy, I think we should go to Portofino, somewhere around there. It should be lovely at this time of year.' France she thought would bring buried memories to the surface and this was not the time to think of the past.

'All right then, you fix it up.'

'Noel, will you come to the Cuthberts tomorrow? I'll need some help getting the chest of drawers home that Madeleine has given to Tammy.'

'Tomorrow? I don't think so. I've got to go to town again. Rather a bore but there's been a problem with the poster I did for the Shakespeare Theatre Group. They want me to do an overlay so I said I'd go by and do it and I can also pick up the tape recorder.'

'Maybe Thursday then?'

'Yes, that would be fine. I'll get the bill.'

Lying. That was a lie. Before last night they were white lies, distortions of the truth, now he was getting caught in a network of absolute untruths. Was she trying to catch him out?

Rebecca linked her arm in his as they left. Their eyes met and lingered on the friendship of the years between them. 'I'm tired,' she said. 'Let's go home and go to bed.'

He could not make love to his own wife. He had never made love to his wife. He looked back over the years to moments of fumbled passion. The difference now was he knew what it was like to make love and be shamelessly loved back. He tried to match Rebecca's face with Briony's sensations and he saw the shapes that he had seen in the car. They were aberrations. He went to the bathroom and took a sleeping pill. Sleep, he thought, would not necessarily make him see it all clearer but it would give him a rest.

THIRTEEN

It was dark when Briony got home. Dark, cold and empty. The only light was the small red flashing one on the answering machine. She didn't want it to be Noel because then she would think about him and that would mean thinking about wanting him to be here, with her. But she was already thinking about him, even if she was thinking she didn't want the message to be from him. So what difference did it make?

She turned on the news and the kettle. Both sounds filled the room, the television with purpose, the kettle with impending domesticity.

Marcus had left the first message. 'Where was she?' He phoned her so often she could not disappear for a night without his knowing. She quite liked that, someone looking after her. Then Noel, the bastard. He wasn't talking to her at all just the machine, apologizing for not taking it too. Taking the machine to a hotel. Noel had names for the machine. Today it seemed to be Flo, he was treating it as he would a cleaning lady.

'All right now Flo, you go and make a cup of tea and I'll talk to your mistress. Hello love,' he said. Here was her burden of guilt. If they shared everything then she must share consequences with him. Briony hated it when he used the word Rebecca. Wife was bad, Rebecca was worse. Had he phoned to leave her with the image of him with someone else as if it was her fault, his situation? The deeper they became involved, the more Rebecca surfaced. His message made her want to see him, to talk to him. She would never phone. Tomorrow, she could see him to clear this slate. For her conscience she had to wipe away distaste. Her thoughts of Noel were soft and comfortable, but his phoning to pass his other life onto her was not fair. As if he knew, he added an afterthought, surrounded by a chuckle and imitation of a tit, bulltit, he said, the warbling he embarked on. Chirpy, chirpy, chirp. 'This is the end,' he said and hung up.

She went to the piano to play and play, to play him out of her. As she ran her hands up and down the keyboard she felt his hands as he had run them up and down her. All right she would gloat on him, get him out that way and she played a slow movement full of feeling. She thought of his arms that seemed so long as they wrapped and wrapped around her, the whiteness of his skin that was firm and muscular, his hair, what was left of it. He was not tall but she loved his height, nor was he particularly well-shaped but she felt he had been moulded especially for her. His words, they caressed her too, he understood and he listened. It was no good, when she finished playing he was still there.

Marcus told her to come over, she could not bear to dwell on 'him' any longer. She went but didn't stay long. Just long enough for someone else to nudge out Noel's continual presence. She went to bed early to sleep without dreams.

The phone was ringing. 'I can't talk for long,' he said. 'How about four o'clock, on the bridge?'

'No, I told you I have a lesson. Five-thirty on the bridge.'

'I have to go,' he said. 'I'll phone the machine and tell you where to meet me.'

She had trained herself not to panic. To long for something so vague. She had always trusted him, but she did not trust herself, the day, the many elements that could still make their meeting go wrong. But her day was hers, until five-thirty, and she did put him away, out of sight until much later.

Once, when they had just met, they used the machine for a rendezvous. He phoned many times a day and when Briony was out she had stopped at a phone booth wanting to hear his voice.

She knew the message by heart because he had left it several days ago and she had not recorded over it. He was on a particularly good roll, impersonating W. C. Fields. But she hadn't expected the next message. I am in town, it said, I'll be at the pub at seven o'clock, I'll wait for you.

By chance it had worked. The many factors that could so easily have prevented them from meeting never arose.

FOURTEEN

It was cold on the bridge, watching the murky river. The water, the sky, the bridge were all the same colour, an impenetrable grey.

It was so tenuous, intangible their hope. Noel caught the eye of a passerby wondering what he was doing. It was too cold to loiter or busk. The smoke from his cigarette and steam of his breath were absorbed by the light layers of fog as they touched the air. He was there alone feeling as grey as the penetrating damp seeping through his clothes.

He began to wonder if she had got his message. At first he attributed her lateness to miscommunication, but as time went on, he started to contemplate the unspoken words between them. Yesterday, the guilt he had inflicted on her, had she taken it as remorse?

As he stood there he felt her around him like the fine notes of a perfume, wafting in and out of the breeze. All he thought he wanted was the soft skin of her cheek to brush against his.

After an hour, he was convinced she had not got his message. He went to phone again, and changed the meeting place to somewhere warmer, a pub at the end of the bridge.

The phone didn't work. She panicked. There was another around the corner. She ran. It was for 999 calls only. She dialled. She lied, but it was an emergency, it was the most precious thing in the world, which she might lose if she did not get through. It rang, her number, once, twice and then the message.

She held her beeper to the phone and pressed the button. But the beeps continued without activating the tape. 'Come on, come on machine,' she said, but the message finished and the machine beeped, one long high squeak and then her breath in uneven pants was recorded. She ran on to find another phone. This next required a phone card. They were not reliable and she prayed before feeding hers into the telephone. The message came on again, with all her might she willed the answering machine to release the message she so wanted. It wouldn't. There was nothing she could do. The machine defied her, it would not tell her where Noel was.

There was only one answer. She must go home, and play back the messages herself if she wanted to find him.

Another taxi but money on love was money well spent. She always spent on presence of mind but now she was swamped with anxiety. It was six o'clock when she unlocked her door, feeling poised, but full of venom towards the machine, its red light signalling messages. He had phoned, he was waiting on the bridge, he'd been there since five-thirty! She shot a look of daggers stabbing at the machine. She ran out, the traffic would be bad, a premonition of how impotent it would make her feel made her heart race.

Noel had waited until six-thirty-five and then walked the length of the bridge to find a telephone. He got the machine again and told it to straighten up, he was so sure that it was playing up. He left it the new venue and dared it to defy him.

Briony could see there was no one on the bridge when she got there at a quarter to seven. She knew the outline of his form, even in the pale dusk. She could not bear it. To go home, without him. To go home unable to phone, to tell him what had happened. She thought of him, driving home, away from her, unsure of when they'd meet again. Hurt, pain, the frustration, knotted themselves into a jagged ball that bounced from her throat to her stomach, pounding in her brain where the hollow behind her eyes ached from unshed tears. 'Noel' she sobbed as she broke down to watch her tears fall from the bridge into the heartless Thames. She toyed with the idea of ringing the machine again but thought it would only be worse, if again she couldn't get through. She turned to go home, but the bridge seemed to welcome her and changing her mind, she walked its tarmacked path to the pub at the end where she asked for the telephone.

'Oh God, Oh God!' whoever you are, whatever you are, please, please don't let him be driving home. It rang, it answered, it worked. There was his voice, strained, worried, but before she heard what he said, she saw him, sitting alone with the last sip of beer.

'Had trouble with the ivories!' he said as he saw her. He kept his smile to keep things simple as he took in the dried tears on her cheeks, her cold hands, her heart pulsing in time with his own. They clung to each other and when he saw her face he captured forever the complex network of emotion that bathed each shadow in light, filled her eyes with wildness, silenced her lips in a tremor.

She was at once tired and limp, relieved of wanting him. Noel watched vowing to capture this moment in his memory, but then he became obsessed with those in his life who needed him. At first he saw Rebecca as she would be when he told her he was leaving. Then Briony without his love, Tammy, the house, the garden, the country.

'I think a brandy is in order,' and, quite unlike him to show affection in public, he pulled her towards him, running her hair through his fingertips and pressing his lips into hers.

That night was spent on the tip of nerves, bubbling and fussy between conversation and hysteria. Tiredness, adrenalin and wine mixing a powerful cocktail. It was no wonder that when Noel slipped briefly into reality, to look at his watch, the hands failed to reassure him. 'We must run. I'll miss the last train.' The bill, coats, taxi, train, and there it was neatly pulling out of the station.

As he went to phone, the drab rows of platforms drove into Briony, what was she doing here, in someone else's life with someone else's man. She felt the neon light pinpoint the hint of a blemish, a line under her eye, the first wrinkle. The dust nestled in her sheer tights, her shoes as worn as the station's concrete. Without the force of Noel's arm in hers she would have left. Gone home to the security of her pretty patterned bedroom with the all cotton sheets and Eric the pink stuffed snail.

Noel had phoned Rebecca, he owed her that, at least, to tell her he'd missed the train. He left Briony standing there, on the cold platform with a few dishevelled commuters catching their last train where she felt self-conscious, as if a huge label hung around her neck, with her name, Adulteress, on it. She looked at Noel for reassurance but he was turning over the same thoughts which were hanging between them. Outside the air was hanging too, caught in the damp web of fog. They waited for a taxi to take them out and quickly wipe the station away.

'I'll put the fire on,' Briony said, letting go of Noel's hand for the first time since the station. As she turned on the gas fire, the warmth of her flat, the lights, her perfume, smothered him and again he felt free from earlier lies.

'Hello, little machine, how are you? Got something to tell us,' Noel acknowledged the flashing light. It was his message, when he phoned from the pub.

He changed his tone. 'Don't you ever do that again. We love you, Briony and I, we trust you, but if you do that again, that's it, your mistress will unplug you and I won't ever talk to you again.' He turned it off with a heartless flick of its knob.

'I'd better take it to be repaired.'

'No,' Noel could not stop himself, if she did that he couldn't phone her, worse still, who would he talk to, if he needed, at a certain time, consolation, reassurance, the machine was always there, he would miss it.

'There's nothing wrong with it.'

'Noel, the thing didn't retrieve my message, we nearly missed each other, it tore at our hearts. There must be something wrong, a loose wire, a small fault somewhere?'

'Don't you see how it controls us?'

'Noel, my love, calm down, it's just a machine.'

'No it isn't. Can't you see that. It was a machine but we haven't treated it like one. We've brought it up, included it with us, fed it doubt, and fear, longing, wishes and hope and it's picked some of them up and thrown them back at us. We can't trust it, it's jealous.'

'It's a machine, Noel.' For the first time she felt she wasn't being honest with him. His words hit truth, but if they both admitted the machine was no longer an ordinary machine that hadn't worked, she feared the consequences.

'I'll take it to the telephone shop and see what they say. There might be a quite logical explanation. I'll borrow another one while it's away. Don't worry, it won't cut us off from each other for long.'

With her eyes that he loved to fall into, full of promise, he saw another conversation. It is dangerous but we must never let it find out we know that.

'Let's have a hot chocolate and a cognac before we go to bed.'

FIFTEEN

This time, the house had missed Noel. As darkness and fog cloaked the secluded countryside, obliterating the day, Noel's presence was sadly lacking. Tammy noticed it, Rebecca sensed that. It had thrown an uneasy feeling into the evening, that neither the smells of cooking, or the buzz of television had removed.

As the hours ticked by she felt her digestion working overtime, linked no doubt to intuition that Noel would miss his train. When he phoned, to confirm what she already knew, it was almost a relief. She could go to bed, without that hint of a thought that he might come home to keep her awake. She hadn't said anything, except 'Yes, dear. No, dear', no point. Instead she vowed to herself to book their holiday tomorrow. If her life was to crumble, she'd rather it was in pleasant surroundings, away from Tammy, when she had a drink in her hand. If they went next week they'd have two weeks before Sophia's party. She didn't want to miss that.

Sophia was an unlikely friend for Rebecca but their differences had wound each other into a common thread over the last few months. Rebecca found herself conspiring, sharing Sophia's secrets and offering advice or consolation. One day Sophia acknowledged her trust and suggested they meet, the three of them, somewhere quite discreet. She picked a glorious day when the best of London was on show. Rebecca had been to Pinewood Studios to drop off her costumes which were met with glowing praise. The compliments stayed with her through the tube journey right to the doors of Brown's where they were meeting for tea.

For a brief moment she saw the intimacy between Sophia and David as they sat so close they seemed to touch each other from foot to shoulder.

'Rebecca,' said Sophia breaking loose. 'This is David.'

'Hello,' they shook hands and his warm smile turned him from a covert lover to a well-mannered, charming man. Yes, already, she thought, she could see the attraction.

He was shy and adored Sophia paying attention to her needs, a sugar lump, hot water in the teapot. He talked, not of himself, but of them, so the conversation was more about stories than opinions. That did not mean of course that he did not have views but he hinted rather than enforced them so that it was tea in every way, calm, and pleasant with no extremes.

It had done her good, Rebecca thought, as she left them. A day of her own. The morning filled with her work, the afternoon, her friends, both having no connection with Noel. She had a number of friends in London who had given up asking her to meet them. It would do her good, she thought, to renew such friendships. If the director liked the costumes she would have more work, which would mean she'd have to come to London regularly.

As she walked by Fenwick's a black knit dress caught her eye. She spun through the doors up to the department on the first floor. Sometimes the mirrors depressed her at that moment when dimpled skin poked out over the top of tights, or from bra straps during their brief exposure as old clothes were exchanged for new. Today she didn't hesitate nor did she have a chance to blame an ill-fit on her figure because the dress clung to her perfectly, hugging and falling quite naturally with striking effect. She strutted outside the changing room to the main showroom, tossing a scarf over her shoulders, trying on a large cardigan.

'I'll take the dress and the scarf' and as an afterthought added the cardigan to her bulky parcel. As she wrote out the cheque a strange jumble of thoughts rested on her maiden name.

For the first time since their meeting over a year ago they did not make love before they slept. They fell asleep in each other's arms at exactly the same time, as if the strains of the day had tired them out equally.

Their conversation lay unfinished around them. Briony's cheek was pushed up close against Noel's flurry chest, a cross between furry and fluffy she called it.

Usually Briony slept in a ball, especially when it was cold. One arm would be under her in a nook between her waist and the sheet while the other was outstretched. Her knees would be crouched into her chest, the bedclothes up to her nose. Noel slept on his back to start with and then would turn onto his side, as if in his sleep he would worry about snoring. He hated to snore. Once Briony had told him, had imitated, his snoring when he had gone to bed drunk. It really was a terrible noise. He'd lain awake after that and caught her making a sort of clucking noise, equally unattractive. When they were even, it became a joke.

When Noel woke up at 4.15 a.m. she was sleeping peacefully. Lured under the covers they had slipped down the slope of pillows without unravelling. A small digital clock radio glowed in the dark, making a fluttering noise as each minute flipped by. He could hear the hum from the refrigerator in the kitchen, elsewhere it was quiet.

He closed his eyes to think, until he was aware of a wet sensation from his throat to his ear. His eyes suddenly open, showing his surprise, came against hers as she melted her lips into his to play with his tongue. The feeling he felt was submission. If he had a white flag, he would wave it. But she had already pinned him down as she climbed on top, freeing his lips, as she looked over him. He had nothing to say and she took his silence as a licence to do what she wished to please.

SIXTEEN

The boiler made a number of low thumping grunts and sent vibrations through the house. It had been doing this for a number of weeks now and still Noel hadn't got it fixed. The shudders were so bad this time that the cupboard door in Rebecca's bedroom sprang open, banging on the wall forcing her out of a deep sleep.

She had overslept, quite out of character, and started rushing her routine, which was usually slow and meticulous. Tammy had already gone to school and left a note.

'Bye Mum. Didn't want to wake you so took the bus. See Ya later.'

Not a word from Noel, which strengthened her resolve. She did without breakfast, scanned the cupboards in the kitchen, took the dry-cleaning and went out.

She drove to the village to buy necessities, drop off the cleaning and find Mr Mann the boiler man, who was nowhere. She left a note for him at the post office and then went to Bury St Edmunds, the nearest big town, for her weekly shop and to visit the travel agent.

In retrospect she wished she had booked the Hotel Splendido but it was almost double the four-star hotel she chose. By the time she added up the airfares, car rental and spending money it seemed too much. But once she felt familiar with the cost of a holiday, which was about half-way home, she doubted her decision. Perhaps Noel will suggest changing it, she thought. There would still be time.

She saw the light in the studio as she turned into the gates. She didn't like to disturb him but at this moment she held no respect for what he was up to. As a compromise, she took him a cup of coffee.

'Hello, love.' Her words were dismissed by a thundering splodge of paint that hit the canvas exactly on target. The paint had branched out to form tiny hands and a million faces. Noel backed into her as he stepped back to admire it.

'Hello, love,' he said.

'Noel, what are you doing?' she asked.

'Good, don't you think, right at the top there.' He had started playing around with the wet paint, moulding it into the shape he wanted.

'What is it?'

'It is the beginning of the paintings I hope to show. A combination of landscape and portrait. It's taking shape. Still a long way off but I know I am pioneering something here. Look, I'm sorry about last night. I drank a bit too much really. Started chatting, you know me.'

'What do you think?'

'Well, I don't know. I like the colours, the shapes, some of those shapes remind me of something but I can't think what it is.'

'I've booked our holiday, two weeks in Italy, leaving next Saturday. That will give us enough time when we get home before Sophia's party.'

Did she make it up, did Noel turn white before he tightened the grip on his brush and fought for excuses? No, she watched his mind flash in and out of thought sequences until he was forced to reply.

'I must go to the toilet.'

Noel was prone to some quite unusual shifts in mood, quirks, eccentricities, paranoia but Rebecca thought this inconsistent even with his inconsistencies.

When he returned, quite flushed she thought before the

connotation struck her as a little too apt, he apologized and thought it was a lovely idea.

'Let's talk about it this evening. I'll leave you to work now, see you later.'

In fifteen minutes he'll be on the phone, she thought, proud that she had accepted Noel's deceit, hoping she would be wrong.

To compose himself Noel opened one of his sketchbooks and looked at the drawings. It was filled with short sentences and many small sketches, something he saw, something he liked, something that came from nowhere. His eye fell upon an insular line which he knew to be Briony's leg and he filled out the shape exactly.

She would calm him down, he'd better talk to her, he was in a state. He dialled her number wary that the machine did not answer, it always did after two rings. Perhaps it was four rings, she'd changed it to four, but four rings had rung by then and the phone wasn't answered. Ten rings he gave it next, then fifteen, seventeen.

The day was ruined.

An electronic dribble was Rebecca's sign. She tiptoed, for no reason, to the phone, a sign of her deceit perhaps, and gently lifted the handset. It rang and rang and rang so she was forced to wait until Noel hung up for fear of a click on the line. She broke down, with silent tears at first then she sobbed convulsively for a long time until she was unsure of what to do next. To carry on or talk to him about it.

SEVENTEEN

By seven o'clock Noel was too restless to sleep. Briony hated that, knowing in his mind he was already on the train making his excuses, finding a way to explain abused fidelities.

Their coffee would be unfinished when he left her with unspoken sentences lying on her lips. Her sad thoughts would be filled with the exhaustion of the day. At first she would feel full of him but later tiredness would leave her susceptible to irritation and tears.

She liked to have something to do that occupied her time without taxing her mind. She decided to take the answering machine to be repaired. With luck, she'd get back with a replacement and he'd never know the difference.

The phone rang. Her first thought was it's him, in a phone booth, he's changed his mind but she knew it wasn't. The abandoned answering machine was eyeing her. She picked up the phone hoping to be thrown back into a normal day.

'Oh! It's you, the real McCoy not the machine.'

'Hello, Marcus, I'm in a flap, no not a flap, confused, although I'm not really no . . .'

'Hungry,' he said, 'or you will be.'

'Am I?'

'Sounds like it. How would you like to play a few pieces at a very fashionable lunch party in two weeks' time? It's something I'd like to take you to and I think it would be an excellent showpiece. The people there are all the types sitting on committees that might get you a grant, or sponsor you in the future. It would be good exposure.'

'Well I think that sounds like something I should think about and say yes,' she said, each word drawn out in line with her rather hesitant thinking, uncertainty crackling down the line.

'Hello? Earth to Briony. Shall we discuss it over lunch. One o'clock, Martino's, in the bar?'

Briony felt the tugging of conflicting responses. 'Yes, super,' she said, 'I'll meet you there.'

She liked to see Marcus after Noel. Always surprises, all at the lightning speed he moved at. The machine, she thought. To get to the restaurant she'd take the tube but the phone shop was quite a walk in the opposite direction. I know, I'll take it with me and get Marcus to drive me home. Noel will be nearly home by now, her thoughts deviated. I'll practise, two uninterrupted hours, half an hour to change, no breakfast, and she went to adjust the piano stool.

The idea of playing at this lunch, to an audience filled her with romantic notions of Mozart playing a Viennese recital. She saw the immaculate clothes, pink and yellow silk, the wigs, Mozart sitting on his piano stool, throwing out the tails of his coat, pausing until the whispers stopped and then his fingers dancing on the keyboard, applause, a commission, recognition. Then the butterflies started. She felt the silence before the music, eyes behind her watching, ready to criticize and felt her heart step up its pace. The music would take over, she was convinced of that, and she would practise what she would play over and over again so she could start automatically without fear blanking out her mind. She would play Mozart and Chopin and maybe, if she felt confident, she would play the Rachmaninov piece. She blew an invisible layer of dust off the keys and started to play.

The music filled the room and cleared her mind. Even Noel was far away. Over and over she played the passages where she would hang too long on one note, not long enough on another, stopping and starting countless times until her dissatisfaction was minimal. Then at last she played the piece all the way through to the end.

She went to change, dressing with care even putting on a bit of lipstick which she only wore for special occasions. Lip gloss she found made her blend into a crowd better and she hated to drink out of a glass with the imprint of lipstick stain. She was looking forward to seeing Marcus. Maybe she could bear the infrequent meetings with Noel she honestly thought, unaware of the lies to herself.

Noel and she always ended up in rather seedy restaurants that they found charming. Blinded by each other a suburban café with strong, lorry driver tea and stained formica table tops would seem conjured up just for them in its perfection. Once they had stayed in a London hotel at some extortionate price to find the room coated in dust with wallpaper peeling and disintegrating around the damp infested areas. Noel had poked a particularly bad patch, where mushrooms were growing, and a huge chunk of crumbling plaster fell on him. They had laughed until pain cramped their stomachs. Noel had insisted on phoning 'the Manager' to complain but he had conveniently gone home. There was no one who seemed to be in charge so Noel asked for the bridal suite as compensation, but was fairly sure they didn't have one. Nobody was going to do anything about it, that soon became apparent, so he ran a bath and the tap fell off in his hand. But there on a lumpy mattress and squeaky spring frame they had announced their feelings to all the neighbouring rooms. Now if they spoke the name of the hotel they would laugh about it together.

Martino's was slick. The waiters wore black with full-length white aprons. They all had black hair and Italian smiles. It was one of those restaurants with thick cotton tablecloths, a huge dessert trolley and a wine waiter with folds of jowls. Signora she was now, wondering whether the transition from Signorina had been to do with age or respect.

Briony liked the way an army of waiters would rush to the door. 'May I take your coat?' they'd ask but their firm hands would have slipped it off before she could answer.

She liked double standards, Noel did too and so did Marcus. She was late again and as a habit went to turn on the machine before she went out. 'Oh no, young man,' she said, 'you're coming with me.' She wrapped its wires and plug and put it in a big canvas bag.

Noel had rung just as Briony was contemplating the dessert trolley. Noel was in a frenzy of distraction while Briony was thinking how good-looking Marcus was. Noel was stone cold sober and going on holiday. Briony decided to have a Sambuca. She was excited about the recital and thought it appropriate to celebrate. She didn't want to leave, she was warm, full and flirtatious.

When she did leave, it was without her canvas bag. She barely heard the chorus of Italian waiters as they poured out of the restaurant with her precious charge. She thanked them many times and hugged the machine to her, feeling her good spirits wilt as she thought of Noel trying to phone. Poor machine, she'd been unnecessarily harsh, she must take it to the shop, buy it a new tape.

Marcus waited while they tested the machine. It worked perfectly each time retrieving and relating messages. The machine had been having her on, she knew it. She thanked the telephone mechanic and buzzed inside with anger at being outwitted.

'You're not going to work now?' Marcus asked her as they reached the flat.

'Come over to the boat, I'll drive you back later.'

'All right, just wait a minute, I'll be right down.'

She ran upstairs with the disgraced machine and plugged it in without ceremony. 'Don't you ever do that again,' she said pointing her finger at it.

Noel felt forced to decide. He knew he couldn't have both. There was no choice if he had to choose. If he had to think about it, he had already decided on Rebecca. It was all a gamble. What could he be sure of? Nothing, a thought which emphasized his sense of doom.

That was why he didn't want to talk to either of them, he wanted the machine. He'd been phoning all day, ever since Rebecca told him about the holiday. He needed someone to talk to. At four o'clock the line was busy. A spark of hope, he waited ten minutes, it might be Briony who answered, he thought, with concern. The dial tone rang, and rang. Half an hour later he phoned again. Click he heard the machine's spools and closed his eyes with relief as he listened to the hum of the tape setting itself up.

'Aha, machine, you're back! Go out for the day, did you? Ha! Stand up an old friend. I'm in a fix,' he said. 'Between you and me and the goalpost. That's it,' he said, triggered by revelation. 'I can see the goal but I've got to kick the ball in to get it, kick the ball hard and that's going to hurt someone. Keep this to yourself you know, the way you do sometimes but, I'm going on holiday, the Italian Riviera. Rebecca went out this morning and booked it. Wants to get me in a confined space, find out what's going on, as if I know. I must get on with my work, away from diversions. I'm doing some of the best work I've ever done.'

He spoke at length about the painting which was sapping his strength, trying to explain it was his soul that was coming out on the canvas.

He loved the way the machine never answered back. It just listened. He felt good hearing out loud the conflict within him. The machine always seemed to understand, he could feel it digesting the information. Sometimes it would throw out a different kind of silence and Noel knew he had gone too far. The machine was developing feelings, Noel sensed it, and admired the machine's ability to stay on an even keel. It never complained. Noel was feeling much better. Maybe the holiday wasn't altogether bad as long as he didn't get ill. He was always worrying about succumbing to some foreign bug.

'Tell Briony I'll give her a ring later,' he told the machine, when he felt calm enough to do some work.

'Right, well I'm signing off now. Bye.' He hung up.

Rebecca realized she was standing, dazed, with her eyes fixed on the telephone handpiece. She had lifted the phone half way through Noel's conversation to hear him talking to a machine. He didn't seem keen on the holiday. That was an understatement. Thank God she'd booked it. Maybe he was having a nervous breakdown. Her disbelief, incredulity, turned to smouldering comfort as she thought maybe he wasn't having an affair after all. Noel was always a little off centre but she put that down to his artistic temperament. Maybe he was nuts. Her mind jumped back to the time she and Noel had been taken to a baseball game in New York. Noel's friend was trying to explain the rules. She'd forgotten most of them except some of the pitching terms. One was a curved ball which was roughly the equivalent of a googly. That's what Noel had done. He'd thrown her a curved ball.

Fortunately for Noel, she had hung up before he mentioned Briony.

The machine had made Noel feel much better. It never forced ideas on him but he heard innuendos, quiet suggestions, through the silences. He was concerned about his work. Briony had become the catalyst he needed to get him out of the rut he called mediocrity. He could do it on his own, but he had wasted time finding excuses, wrestling between commercial trivia and art. He had woven a web of responsibilities each one drawing him further and further into a net. The house, the heating bill alone made him shudder. Tammy's school fees, health insurance: the list was endless. Before he met Briony he had signed a contract with a conglomerate which made earth moving vehicles, subway cars and all sorts of bulldozer type machines. The money was too good. Early discussions over a casual lunch had turned to a boardroom, he wished he'd never taken it on.

Often he would look out of the window. He could see for miles, a collage of tall, wavering trees, reaped fields, a stray farmhouse drenched in dew in the early morning and dry in the evening after a day's sun. Sometimes he drifted to the barren scenery of his childhood. Then he would try to think back to his earliest memory. Each time it was the same. He must have been four when his mother gave birth to a stillborn child. He had forced this memory so often that he could sense the smell of the hospital, the squeak of the wheels on the stretchers, the colour of blood in plastic bags. Now he didn't know if he remembered the hospital that time or if it was a year later when she died.

At first he had wanted to be a pilot, he always loved flying, whether it was away from himself into a land of make-believe or with all the fine tuning of mechanics. His father had been a watchmaker. He used to let Noel dabble with clocks, taking each tiny mechanism to pieces and then fixing it up again. Noel was deft with his hands and soon learned the mechanics. Then he tired of the tiny mechanisms and would draw each detail in case he lost a piece and couldn't remember where it went. His drawing soon took over and swayed within extraordinary dimensions so that the clock would become unrecognizable in the maze of colour and shapes that invaded the page.

He was six when the war ended casting its repercussions on the shape of his life. He was lucky, his stepmother had pushed for him to go to art school.

Noel's first published drawing had appeared in *Gazebo* magazine in 1956. It was more like a cartoon than a drawing. The news had covered a manufacturer of gardening tools whose faulty product had got them a headline. Noel had caricatured a gardener who accidentally cut off his hand with a shovel when it became separated from its handle. One newspaper bought the copyright to reprint his drawing with their story so he got some money and rare coverage. From this he managed to sell a few one-offs to various publications until he found a small publisher to print his first children's book. *The Man in the Moon gets Married* was lapped up by adults and children. It was made into a television film and syndicated worldwide. He still got royalties from it now. He did sequels at the time and then was asked by a major publishing house to illustrate *The Hobbit* by Tolkien.

For this he changed his life, entering what he called his 'living on the edge' period. He travelled to feed his imagination and came back to work on it continuously for nearly a year. What he read into the characters and Tolkien's descriptions showed 'an unparalleled talent' or so the critics said. They were all agreed on his chances of becoming a real artist with time and experience.

Noel had his first television interview as a result of a publisher's publicity campaign when he went down on file as 'good material'. It was rare for an artist to be associated with a sense of humour, to be considered good value on air and this worked in his favour.

His next project was to illustrate and live out *Zen and the Art of Motorcycle Maintenance,* which took him on a path that led to his first wife.

EIGHTEEN

Briony was convinced Marcus did not live on the houseboat. There were too many inconsistencies and not enough room. He often smelt as if he'd been soaking in Badedas and he couldn't do that on the boat. Where did he keep his clothes?

She had never pried because she wanted to keep their friendship quite open. Confidence built on intimate secrets later became bargaining tools, so she liked to be friendly but not personal. Their familiarity was gradually breaking down such barriers. Already she was aware of a growing closeness between them and with the wine inside her, the antennae which usually paid attention to such things wavered.

Marcus opened a bottle of Calvados and kept her alert with a shot of Espresso. He was intrigued by her loyalty to Noel. Briony was aware of this and regretted the one time when she had introduced them. At the time she couldn't see any alternative. She and Noel spent so little time together that when he phoned for a chance meeting she was already committed to seeing Marcus. She had wondered how he would take it when she showed up with Noel, but he didn't seem to have minded and the three of them had spent the evening together.

Marcus had noticed the magnetism between them, their eyes speaking a silent language, and when they touched, the air seemed to fold in around them, protecting them. He found such attraction fascinating, wishing to uncover their secret so that he could have it too. He found himself getting too fond of Briony, knowing a friendship would last longer, trying to change his mind. But as he sat, listening to her laugh as she wrapped her legs around the cushions, sipping her drink, leaving its wetness glistening on her lips, cocking her head from side to side, he longed to kiss her. Several times their lips had brushed when he kissed her cheek but clipped the side of her mouth and they had caught each other's eye with a glance of embarrassment.

He decided instead to take her into the computer cave, where fluorescent lights bobbed and flashed, in synchronization with the chatter of clicks, hums and bleeps. The occasional print-out would roll neatly into a tray, the fax line would ring and click on.

'What are they all, Marcus? What do they do? Are you masterminding an international satellite link, peering into people's drawing rooms? Perhaps you're a spy. Or are you dealing in computer money? Buying and selling all over the world in different time zones, cashing in on commodities?'

Her laugh as she said this echoed around the room, bouncing off the screens. He caught the mischief in her eyes and laughed too.

'Nothing quite as far-fetched,' he said. But it was.

Each terminal locked into a system with outlets all over the world so he could, at any time, make contact with many places in most countries. In some less developed countries he had devised simpler communication networks to deliver a message.

The room was divided into continents with each corner representing chunks of the world. At various times of the year, Marcus received payments which he divided up in the most tax efficient way before dispersing them amongst the one million and thirty-seven charities his network supported. If he was, for example, contributing to a tree planting scheme in Guinea he would provide the actual seedlings rather than money which sometimes got caught up in bureaucratic man-handling. So as to constantly earn maximum interest he would dabble in financial markets making best use of whichever currency was strong at the time.

'You what? I don't believe it.' Briony felt the effects of the Calvados slipping way with the force her concentration demanded to take in Marcus' explanations.

He tapped on a keyboard to show multiple donations to Cancer Research and how it had been kept anonymous. Bit by bit Briony grasped a few rudiments of this complicated process.

What Marcus refused to tell her, was where the money came from. She pleaded and tormented him in an attempt to prise out this piece of the puzzle. But he remained firm and she ever inquisitive.

Late night had set in by the time Marcus drove Briony home. The streetlights shone on the road while the windscreen wipers drew their rubber blades over the glass, making the only noise. Occasionally another car would swish by.

She could sense the peaceful breathing of sleep all around her, the loneliness of night without its revellers. Marcus was quiet, looking far beyond the road. She felt his shield of betrayed confidence. He had told her his secret and her responses fell short of his expectations. She had lost that precious moment by her caution and now it knotted the air between them severing their closeness in the car by distance.

'Marcus, I . . .'

'It's all right.'

'No, you're wrong. I do understand. It was overpowering, such a surprise to find I knew so little about you that now I realize I know even less.'

'Don't talk about it Briony, not tonight. It's late, you're tired and emotional,' he said, his lips curling to a smile, breaking his frozen disappointment.

'I'm taking it too seriously. It's just that I haven't told anyone about it before. It's been a secret for so long.'

They had reached her flat and Marcus went to open her door.

'No, don't come up. We're both tired. Tomorrow you will see

that through my eyes it is an overwhelming honour, I am very moved by what you did, I am grateful for our friendship.'

As she reached to kiss him goodnight he was there fighting for control, resisting their mutual attraction.

The answering machine tugged at her like guilt, playing on her sensitivities. She knelt over it hoping the flashing red light would hypnotize her, dry her tears, take her away. Then softly, succumbing to its power, she pressed the button.

For once the machine took pity and with vigour fastwound its spools so that Noel's conversation was replayed in full.

She felt tension at once: something was wrong, she was eavesdropping, it was not hers, this conversation. She felt anger rise bristling in her skull behind the sockets of her eyes. His breach of loyalty. His news hit her next, wriggling about in the seed of her doubt. He was going away with her, not her Briony, her his wife, and again she felt the anger protecting her sudden sense of loss. Silently her tears fell as she sat crumpled on the floor and listened to the rest.

He woke her up, speaking tentatively, when she dealt him the tone of her voice, and tried at once to make amends.

The vague nightmare flitted between her dreamier thoughts and waking reality. Her eyes stung from tiredness and her stomach fluttered like wind whipping up in a tunnel.

Noel felt her tiredness and wished he could be there.

'I am sorry my dearest one but Rebecca arranged this holiday without my knowing anything about it. It is not unusual for a man and wife to go on holiday once a year.'

He could hear his words plop like heavy stones on a lake and lie deep in her silence.

Briony tried to revive herself by humming arpeggios in her head.

'I know, Noel. It's not that, you know it isn't.'

'I know,' he said.

'When are you going?'

'Saturday.'

'That's less than a week.'

'Yes. I must see you before. There are things I want to tell you which I cannot do on the phone.'

'My love,' she said, bracing herself for what she found so disturbing, 'you had no trouble talking on the phone yesterday.'

'You were out all day, you took the machine with you. At least when you are not there I can talk to the machine but it wasn't there.'

'I think the machine should be called Adolph,' she said.

'Briony, don't. You love the machine too. Don't you remember how often it's helped us? You wouldn't treat an old friend this way.'

'It knows too much, I think we should get rid of it.'

'Briony no, don't, don't speak like that, it will hear you.'

'Noel, this is ridiculous, it's an answering machine, a malfunctioning answering machine and we're reading too much into it.'

'No it's not. I need the machine.'

'This is absurd.'

'Briony?'

'Yes, Noel.'

'If I wasn't married, you know I would be with you.'

'Would you die for me, Noel?'

'What? Well, yes.'

'How would you do it then?'

'I haven't really thought about it. I suppose I could tie my socks into some sort of noose and rig up a hanging post . . .'

'Not *those* socks.'

'You mean the green ones?'

'It wouldn't be appropriate. Can you imagine Romeo killing himself in his pants?'

'I beg your pardon?'

'Wearing his pants. Just standing there in his underpants. It wouldn't be tragic.'

'All right then. I'll dress up. I'd wear a D.J.'
'You haven't got one.'
'I'd rent one.'
'How would you get it back, you'll be dead?'
'Perhaps you could take it back for me. Besides I don't think, under those circumstances, returning a dinner jacket would be my top priority.
'Would you die for me too?'
'Noel, you know I would.'
'If we both did it at the same time we could forget the dinner jacket! I'm sorry Briony, that conversation with the machine, leaving you out. Will you meet me on Friday, I'll take the train?'
'Yes, you know I will. Shall I meet you at the station?'
'No, stay in bed. I'll wake you up more gently than today.'
'All right, Noel.'
He had turned her around again.

NINETEEN

After breakfast Rebecca wiped down the kitchen table and covered it with a map of Italy. They were to fly to Florence because Noel wanted to go back to the Uffizi and the Galleria dell'Accademia. She had rented a car to drive to the coast then up to Santa Margherita.

The brochure made the hotel look pleasant, but what little excitement she had for the holiday was curtailed by her worries about Noel. He was always pacing, wringing his hands, getting up early, going to bed late and locking himself in the studio for hours at a time. She hoped he wouldn't get ill. Noel was not a natural traveller, disasters were attracted to him and suspect seafood always found his plate.

She liked the idea of having a real tan for Sophia's party and remembered she must get total block for Noel and batteries for his Walkman. He was the only man of his age she knew who used one. She had tried to use it and was surprised to find that Noel taped his favourite movies, the Marx Brothers and W. C. Fields and listened to the soundtrack. He liked pop music but was several years behind the times.

The costumes were going to give her another six months work. For a low budget film the money allocated for wardrobe was generous. She should get another three ready by Friday then she could combine dropping them off with a shopping expedition. It was the end of summer and the sales had started.

At this time of year the Mediterranean would be gloriously warm and the days not too humid. It was the same time of year she had spent with Lou that magical summer many years ago. He had tired of her. Month after month she had thought he owed her an explanation for suddenly breaking her life in two. But she saw him with girl after pretty girl at concerts, in the theatre, and one day when yearning for him had subsided and jealousy had worn her out she realized he could never be happy with anyone for long.

Noel would probably grab a few clothes the night before and pack in a flurry. He always left things to the last minute. At first it would annoy her. Now what infuriated her was that he would always forget things and had to buy them at the inflated prices of resorts, taking up valuable holiday time. This year she would organize herself and if he forgot anything he could go out with the phrase book and replace it.

The week was dragging and the music wasn't sounding sweet. In between scales Briony would stop and remember parts of Noel's conversation with the machine, the intimacy, his confidences. She tried to let her jealousy hide behind simpler feelings of mistrust, but that machine was becoming irksome.

She thought back to the time over a year ago when they first met, how perfect it was, the longing, the sweet untroubled hope. If only that encapsulated moment could have stayed the same but so much had changed because of human failings. Sometimes she would try to convince herself out of him. Take each trait of his character and find fault with a few. But as a whole the faults took on a different light and she knew there was no getting away from it.

Marcus had not phoned since she last saw him. She decided to get in touch, invite him for dinner on Saturday night, she would need a distraction by then.

She got up to make herself a cup of coffee and thought she must get around to phoning a window cleaner. The flat had a whole side of windows in the sitting room leading to a small balcony and french doors in her bedroom. Now they were coated with a film of dirt from the traffic. Although her flat was small it was an oasis, overlooking the Royal Hospital grounds, near the river and an easy walk to the King's Road. Even on rainy days it was light and fresh. A five-foot painting that Noel had given her hung on the wall behind the piano. It was the only oil he had given her. She had a cupboard filled with his posters and mementoes, drawings he did when they were together. She always wanted him to draw something for her that represented their love, just as she had written music for him, but he never had.

Noel phoned her less than usual during the next few days because she was so clearly in his mind. He was painting her with the accuracy of his feelings. Sometimes when they'd met and she was sad, or gay, he sketched her expression, exaggerating it, so his drawing of her was never as important as the moment. He had never drawn any more than that.

It was a long time since he'd used oil. Most of his work he painted on handmade paper using inks or acrylic so he was unfamiliar at first with the texture of oil, and the time it took to dry. He had thought of painting her for many months but was frightened of Rebecca finding out. A large canvas was not easy to hide. Now he didn't care. He was aware of Briony pulling away from him, the shortness of time which lent her to masquerade. If he could read her soul into her nakedness he could immortalize her in paint. If he could do it with her he could do it again because that was the difference between a good painting and an exceptional one.

Rebecca felt tenseness in her neck and shoulders brought on by the nagging list of chores to deal with before the holiday. She wanted to make sure there was enough for Tammy to eat in the freezer and had arranged babysitters and overnight stays with friends. Next year she would leave Tammy on her own, but for this holiday she felt better having one less thing to worry about. Tammy had always been independent, a non-conformist. Rebecca kept reminding herself that Tammy was younger than she looked. Already she noticed the boys hanging around her at school. It was not surprising with her mane of red hair and Rebecca's slim, long, freckled legs. She was clever too and didn't have to work hard to get high marks. She was popular at school, Rebecca was glad of that. How would Tammy take it if she and Noel were to separate? She was still only fourteen. The thought had come, just slipped into her mind. She let it out just as quickly and got on with her work.

To get the costumes ready in time Rebecca worked late most nights. Noel was in his studio. They met for meals but little else and for once she was as preoccupied as he. Neither of them had mentioned to the other their intentions to go to London on the Friday before the holiday.

At lunchtime on Thursday Noel came into the kitchen to make a sandwich. 'I'm going to town tomorrow, to sort out a few things, pick up the traveller's cheques, is there anything you want, love?'

'That's lucky,' Rebecca replied. 'I'm going too. I have to drop off the pink and silver costumes and I thought I'd do a bit of shopping, pick up some suntan lotion and something to protect you. We can go down together.'

'I was going to take the train. It's such hell driving around central London.'

'That's all right,' she said. 'I don't mind going by train.'

'I was going to leave early, to fit everything in, does that suit you?'

'How early, Noel?'

'The 6.40 a.m.'

'Noel, that's crazy. You'd be there by 8 o'clock. Nothing will be open by then.'

'I thought I'd have breakfast with Rory to talk about the

Huckleberry Finn book Rubenstein want me to do. I want Rory to start negotiating.'

'Oh!' she said, thinking she'd probably get the later train, which would mean taking two cars to the station.

TWENTY

Briony usually woke up at seven although she never used an alarm. Today she woke at four convinced she would never go back to sleep. The fridge was humming away and she got up to make a cup of tea, running her hand along the closed lid of the piano on the way to the kitchen. The night seemed to her to beg for music and she would have liked nothing more than to play. The neighbours would like nothing less and it had not been long since they last complained so she settled herself with reading and dreaming of Noel. At about six o'clock she fell headlong into a deep sleep.

The gods had endorsed his secret love, thought Noel, as the train rolled smooth as silk along the tracks to London. Last night Sophia had phoned to ask Rebecca if she wanted a lift into town today. It had worked out perfectly. He had bought fresh roasted coffee yesterday, he would get croissants on the way to her flat and a bunch of flowers, something unusual. Noel was not the kind of man to buy flowers but today, this morning, he wanted it all to be right before he went away.

He took a taxi from the station, made his stop on the way and found the spare key which she kept taped inside her car bumper. The only miscalculation of his silent entry was the pulsing of adrenalin which made his touch uncertain and movements clumsy. He managed to open the door with a small click, tiptoe to the bedroom where to his surprise she was still asleep.

The moments until he was under the cover, touching her

skin, seemed endless. The click of metal as he undid his belt, the ring of his zip as he undressed, he was sure would wake her. He sensed her heat before they touched and felt his longing rise in anticipation of her milky warm skin. He could not decide which part of her he wanted to feel first.

Briony felt his presence as in a waking dream. It was as if he had been there all night and to wake feeling him next to her evoked an excitement confined only in its wickedness. She felt primed and alert running her hand over her body to make sure it was ready. It was lust to which she aspired, there were no words important enough to take her lips away from his when they met, no part too private for his intrusion. She gave him all, without inhibition or modesty. He felt the wait which he held onto, delaying, restraining before lowering himself on her, a sensation which would send him trembling into her source. He could feel her same effort to harness the desire to let go long before they made love. His hands shielded her from the world as he held her face close to his, their eyes meeting, while their tongues lashed and entangled. He saw her powerless to resist, forced to succumb to her only choice. She gave herself up, her flesh rippling in surrender, her nerves to dance, partnering his in delirium. Each finger felt a sensation as she ran her hands and nails over his chest to the soft hollow of his belly, to his pelvis and the clenched muscles of his thighs. She threw her head back, stretching, arching herself towards him, a shameless sacrifice. She wasn't thinking, wasn't feeling because some divine ecstasy had taken over.

The sweat had turned to torrents so heated was their love. They would glide across each other like the blade of a skate over ice, skimming. Her straw coloured hair became glued and matted, standing out from her face like the mane of a wild animal. No kiss went deep enough, but that was good, because there would be another one until finally like a captive balloon on a string they broke loose.

They laughed with relief as no words seemed appropriate.

'Good morning.' 'Good morning.' They said and watched each other's eyes as their wildness calmed and their heat cooled.

They lay for a long time in each other's arms until a restlessness to talk, to settle up, to work out the next two weeks caught up with them.

'Don't get up, I'll make us some coffee.'

She feared his leaving. It had happened so often, his dressing after they made love and then he was gone. Although he was coming back this time, she could only feel him leaving.

'Noel, I've been asked to play, a recital at a garden party. Marcus set it up. What do you think?'

She could hear his feet on the lino.

'You mean playing the piano at a party? Will they be sitting down or milling about?'

'Sitting down. I think there are chairs, I think it will be quite formal.'

'What will you play.'

'Chopin, Mozart, Grieg and maybe Rachmaninov.'

'Will you play it for me now, Briony?'

'But you told me to stay in bed.'

'No, play it now, before you think, while I get us breakfast.'

She needed little encouragement because now she could play. All week she had wanted to play it to him, it was a release to receive his endorsement. She put on a white towelling dressing gown and the ballet shoes she wore as slippers, patted the piano lid and settled herself on the stool.

He could see her hands poised on the notes and then she left him for a while without excluding him.

The music filled the room and he sank between the idle sway of its melody, tossed on the notes until it played with him like a cat's cradle, his concentration momentarily lost then regained.

'Bravo, bravo.' He clapped and kissed her and carried her back to bed.

'It's much better, isn't it?'

'Yes, Briony, it is not the same music you played to me before.

'There's something I want to tell you too, about a painting I am doing, for me, of you.'

'A painting of me? Will I have to pose, will we be like Picasso and his mistress?'

'I don't know, but if I can't paint with you, if I can't make this exceptional then maybe I'll have to accept that I am only mediocre.'

'Noel, don't talk like that, putting yourself down. We both know it's a struggle. Neither of us would be any good without it.'

'Come here.'

His arm seemed to wrap and wrap around her, coiling like a snake with the softness of silk and warmth of security. He played with her lips, possessing her.

'It's important to remember that an artist starts with nothing, just a white surface. A score with no notes. He must begin a dialogue with that white surface, a conversation that fills the page otherwise the white surface stares back with its blankness. He is not the inanimate object, he is the living form. The artist, me, I must find, draw, the first gesture on the page, initiate the conversation and then the dialogue will take on its own form. Neither you nor I will know which way it will go.'

They talked into their world at length while the coffee grew cold and the morning passed. Their words wrapped them tighter to each other the way their bodies had earlier. They paused to touch just lightly which led to time detached in the languid, lazy love they made.

Too soon their time was devoured. They showered together trying to let the force of the water knock in some sense, bring them down to earth. It was almost too natural the way their nakedness made them rub and nudge each other, laughing about nature's curious designs, asking questions adults take for granted.

Noel was at the mirror sucking in his lip to give the razor a taut surface.

'Let me try,' she said, scooping the blade softly up his chin listening to the whiskers crackle then snap off.

'I'm glad I don't have to to that.'

He reciprocated by enveloping her legs in stockings. But he fumbled with his hands pushing and forcing the sheer from her heel where it was irredeemably caught.

'Thank God I don't have to encase my legs in these sheath-like contraptions,' he said.

They went out for lunch and had trouble finding a place still serving. They needed a table between them, the bustle of the waiters to prepare them somehow for Noel's absence. They did not talk once of shallow details. Although she wished him well it was hard to think him happy without her. And he with another, his entangled thoughts seemed hypocritical with her so close.

'I'll come to the station with you,' she said with quiet resign.

'No.'

'It's all right, I want to.'

'No, you can't. Rebecca will be there.'

He had not wanted to say it. Nor had he wanted to lie, to bring her into their last minutes. His words cut into the perfect harmony they had bathed in all day.

So quickly he was changing from her to Her, thought Briony. Not even a train ride to separate them.

His reasons fell limp between them. Already he was on a train, and then a plane far away from her.

'I'll get the bill,' he said.

But she was thinking, he knew all along when he would leave. Not even the flexibility of missing a train and catching another. No chance to change his mind. She pulled the walls of her defence around her so that he felt her stiffen.

He always liked to finish things off. Leave her with a kiss that lingered, words iced with hope. This time he saw he left her nothing and thought he deserved the cause which cut her up.

They tried to flow again within one another but the moment was passed.

'I'll call you,' he said.

TWENTY-ONE

The trains were lined up like ten pins, sloppy guardsmen lolled by the gates, litter danced in wind-tunnels. Rebecca was late, the train was about to leave. Noel sat alone with his thoughts as the train pulled out of the station, watching the platform slip by beside him.

There had been a change of plan. Sophia was to meet her husband at a cocktail party so they could drive home together. But Darwin had woken that morning feeling as if a ten-ton lorry had driven through his throat. He abandoned all plans and left Sophia to her own devices. Rebecca had been more than willing to drive back together and had tried in vain to contact Noel.

She phoned Rory, his agent, who said he wasn't expecting Noel until later and left a message with him. She had lunched with Sophia and David, and drank a little too much wine. The cheque for the costumes padded her pocket and the prospect of sun and a change of scene had lightened her spirits further.

When the train arrived Noel wondered whether to take the car or leave it for Rebecca and take a taxi. He doubted she had keys and chose its comfort. He cursed this cruel twist of fate and found his other life, his real life, not so real at all. He started to play with the consequences of leaving Rebecca but was jarred in his thoughts by Tammy who heard the tyres on the gravel and ran to meet him.

'Hello Daddy,' she hugged him.

'Mummy's bringing a huge cake, which she and Sophia bought. She should be home any minute.'

They went inside and Noel listened to Tammy's chatter. He wanted to pay attention knowing she was nervous about them going away without her.

'On Wednesday I'm going to a party at Erica's. Most of my class will be there and there's going to be dancing. It's her birthday. Dad, can I have a party for my birthday?'

'We'll see about that closer to the time.'

Tammy went to the fridge and offered Noel a lemonade.

'Thanks love, I'll have a beer.'

'There aren't any in the fridge.'

'Can you get me one from the garage then, there's a whole case by the freezer.'

'O.K.' she said, and went to the garage just as Sophia's car pulled up.

Noel heard their high-pitched talk and practised a smile.

'Hello girls,' he said, 'have a good day in town?'

'Yes, lovely, Noel,' said Rebecca. 'You got my message all right. I thought you were seeing Rory first thing so it was lucky that you met up after I phoned.'

'Sophia, can I get you something to drink?' Noel offered, as an excuse to regain his compsure.

'No thank you, Noel. I better get back and see how Darwin is. He's sounding rather poorly. Bye Rebecca, bye Noel, have a lovely holiday. I'll see you at the party.' She turned on her high heels and made for the door which Noel opened.

Rebecca put the large box on the table and collapsed in a chair.

'I'm tired, and I've still got a bit of packing to finish. Have you packed yet, Noel?'

'No, I, well, I was going to do it after supper.'

'I washed some shirts for you.'

'Oh! Thanks, I've rather left everything to the last minute.'

'As usual.'

'Mummy, can I see the cake?' Tammy had dropped her adult guise and was filled with excitement. What simple pleasure, Noel thought.

'All right, but be careful, it's soft and fragile.' Noel's heart jumped.

Tammy carefully unwrapped the box while Rebecca and Noel looked at each other. It was going to be all right, thought Rebecca. He returned her smile and the three of them brimmed with the warmth and comfort of home.

After dinner Noel went to the studio for reassurance more than anything else. He phoned Briony but she was out. He thought she would be, not wanting to be alone, with him going away. He thought about her life and realized he hardly knew her friends.

'I must keep some of my life to myself,' she had told him once, 'otherwise I would be left with nothing or you in everything.' He understood, of course, but what did she do, some of those nights? The gigs she played, the fancy restaurants with Marcus. She was pretty, what man would not want her? How long would she be there for him?

He looked at the painting he had begun and knew it was good and with a hint of nostalgia closed the door and went to deal with the details of the holiday.

Briony took a long bath scented with pine bubbles. They both knew the train had nothing to do with it, they had changed. Once they wanted nothing and now they expected more. They had fallen into the traps set up for every extra-marital lover. She rose from her reveries to add more hot water and turned on her stomach with her hips resting gently on the bottom of the bath, her chin framed by bubbles.

The bath washed away her doubts. Resigned to the hopelessness of it all she dressed carefully to boost her confidence. Tomorrow, she thought, she would take up running. Fine tune her body, something physical would make her sleep better.

She'd train quite ruthlessly. If only she didn't find it quite so boring.

Natalie had given her a piee by Gabriel Grovlez. She got the music and started to sight read. It was a clarinet solo with piano accompaniment. Natalie had someone in mind to play the solo and wanted Briony to accompany him. She thanked the music for absorbing her when the doorbell rang two hours later.

Marcus was wearing a dinner jacket with a crisp white shirt, not one of those ghastly frilly jobs Briony hated. He oozed style and she took pleasure in watching the lilt of his mouth when he smiled. He bowed and produced a bottle of vintage champagne.

'If it suits the lady,' he said, 'it would give me great pleasure to share a little of this champagne.'

'Upon my word,' she said, fighting off a smile, 'the pleasure is all mine!'

He was more relaxed, she thought, relieved since it was the first time she had seen him since the time on the boat.

'I'm glad to see you.'

He popped the bottle and the drink quickly set them at ease.

'How's Noel?' he asked, and Briony's cheeks, dimpled with content, sagged. 'Oh Marcus,' she said, 'I don't know.'

It felt better to talk about it, to shake it out in the open, falling into pitfalls of clichés. Quite sweet, Marcus was, the way he understood, the way he had sensed what it was between them, Noel and Briony, that neither could let go.

Marcus looked at his watch and poured the last of the champagne. 'I've arranged something I think you'll like tonight. But we better go now.'

She let herself he led by his perfect manners to the car. Marcus turned the tape up loud, he had two weeks while Noel was away, he would make sure her tears would stay away until she realized she had shed none.

He took her down a side street, through a mews somewhere behind South Audley Street. A single arch of white fairy lights marked a solid wood door with no number or name on its adjacent entry phone. Marcus rang the bell and they waited until the door was opened by a man in a full length green coat with brass buttons and top hat to match. The steps were narrow and laid in thick red carpet. It seemed a long way down until they reached a padded door. The doorman leaned towards the handle and as he squeezed it open the noise fell out.

Marcus wanted to capture that memory for ever. The way her face lit up, soft orange shades flowing to her cheeks, her hands that leapt in delight to cover the honeyed scream of exclamation. When she turned to him she had bitten her lower lip to contain herself but he could see her jumping inside.

It was a scene of fantasy. It reminded him of Prohibition, the excitement of secrecy, the lights, the clothes, the dancers, the sound of people oblivious to anything but fun. The room fanned like a shell opening at the back to the mass of jungle life which draped the stage. It could have been the Folies Bergère in its prime. Leggy dancers in tiny feathered leotards filled the stage, their headdresses a mass of tall white feathers, under which their Cleopatra eyes beckoned and flirted. They wore stilettos as thin as a wand, walking with elegance and pride, the ripple of muscles between the scanty straps of their body stockings catching the spotlight. The music came from a sunken orchestra. All Briony could see at first was the conductor's baton held in a brilliant white gloved hand. All around the tables sparkled as cutlery and cigarette lighters caught the light. Gold and silver cigarette cases and small exquisite evening bags littered tabletops. At the side of each table coated with thick crimson tablecloths was a silver bucket with ice-cold champagne.

The men were all handsome. Some lean, others well-built, smelling of money, and after-shave. Briony looked at the hairstyles and felt the richness of the black curls on a woman in a backless gold lycra dress, the plaited mane of a lady in clinging black sheath, the wild red flames from a girl with bedroom eyes and a skirt which showed her stocking tops. In her greed to take it all in Marcus had to lead her by the hand to their table beside the stage.

He watched her face. Her eyes drinking it in, breathing in the clothes, the ambience, the faces.

'What would you like, Briony? Some wine?'

His words brought her back where she felt with shyness the magnitude of it all. The lights and colours, the glitter and silent waiters who flowed around the tables.

'Well,' she said, showing her amazement and he acknowledging it. 'Yes that would be lovely.'

While Briony put on airs in her glittering nightclub Noel packed his suitcase. He looked for his shaving cream, knowing as he packed he was not taking the right things. He felt he would never get packing right. He tried to settle his discontent so he could leave without the queasiness in his stomach. It would help if he talked to Briony before they left. He saw the way her eyes had signalled impatience and he blamed himself. He dared not phone the machine and tell it so. He could feel the smell of travel already. The angular patterned carpets at the airport, tearful reunions and farewells, the dirty stand-up ashtrays littered with half-chewed sandwiches and cigarette butts. There was something about the air and authority, the scrutinizing looks of customs officials that made him feel tired before he started travelling. The knowledge that he was only going further and further away from the comforts of his home.

Rebecca was already asleep when he went to bed, scrunched to his side at eye-level with the alarm clock. He tried to shake off nasty thoughts with made-up images of the paintings in the Uffizi and went to sleep in the midst of Michelangelo's statues.

Briony looked as if the night had taken its toll when she got home just after four in the morning. Her clothes smelt of smoke, her hair was flat and uncombed, and her skin drained and sallow. It was still dark but an early morning feeling clawed at the dawn, the end of night fighting to stay up, the beginning of day eager to break out. Methodically Briony wiped off her make-up with cotton-wool balls. She barely had time to look at the wrinkled sheets and remember Noel before she floated through a tunnel to sleep.

The phone was inhuman, so loud, what a vile way to wake up, who could have invented that noise, where was the damn thing? She searched the folds of the duvet which lay on the floor covering the piercing tones that shredded her nerves.
 'Hello, love.'
 There he was sounding small, soft spoken and searching for her approval. She at once felt the contradiction of her mood. Grouchy, irritable, her temper balanced precariously, her voice several octaves lower than usual. Then it hit her, a premonition of loneliness which no late night would dispel.
 'Sorry, Noel. I was out late, with Marcus. Trying to wipe out those ugly moments, before you caught your train. It was never meant to be like this!'
 'Yes, I know, I've been the same. I just phoned . . .'
 'Have you packed?'
 'Yes, I've taken those boxer shorts you gave me, the ones with the monkeys climbing up the Empire State.'
 'Where are you going to say you got those from? They don't exactly blend into the background, especially that one monkey!'
 'I could have bought them.'
 'Noel, do you think you'll be able to phone?'
 'Yes, of course I will. I better go now. I'll bring you back a chime from the Duomo.'
 'Look after yourself.'
 'You too.'
 'Oh wait!'
 'What?'
 'Well?'
 'Nothing.'

They said goodbye again, never wanting to put down the phone, but at the same time wanting to hear the click. They felt a terrible wrenching as they both stayed staring at the walls caught up in that empty moment.

TWENTY-TWO

Rebecca moved as if she had tiny wings fitted to her feet. Like a bat she was at once everywhere, fluttering, tangling herself in every small corner. Now she had homed in on Tammy, clutching lists of phone numbers and spouting instructions.

Tammy had the mischievous look of every adolescent being left on her own for the first time. Parties, smoking: the list of activities usually banned seemed irresistible in their temptation. She was not the type to break rules for the sake of it, but to explore previously denied territory and its thrills had an appeal.

The taxi arrived fifteen minutes early. They always did when you had a long journey ahead, thought Noel. The extra drive from the airport was one of his hates when he moved to the country. Airports were supposed to be handy. He put his sketch book, paints and brushes in his hand luggage together with a clutter of cameras, spying his sunglasses on a shelf at the last minute. His suitcase shut with a hiss of air which tumbled around amongst the ridiculously small number of clothes he had packed. He was wearing his monkey boxers.

The driver was looking at Rebecca as she negotiated the gravel drive in high heels, accentuating her figure in the tight, slim fitting dress she wore. Noel looked at his moccasins, which Briony had said looked like a platypus. He was comfortable in his corduroys and lambswool sweater and the bomber jacket had become an old friend. He was the only one who liked it.

There they were, the two of them in the taxi, off on holiday. They started with the 'got the passports, tickets, money' routine, went over what they might have forgotten and then silence. Rebecca gave Noel her 'you don't have to tell me anything' look and his stomach tightened. They had been married fifteen years and she had filled a large part of his life, there was no reason for everything to end now. With the same gesture as swatting a fly he tried to stop Briony buzzing around him, just for two weeks.

Rebecca relaxed the moment the house was out of sight and sank into the ribbed taxi seat. She found herself going through a checklist with Noel and then tossed her head as if to shake off the part of her which organized. Noel looked a bit glum, she thought, so she teased him with the guidebook and ploughed his thoughts with the feast which lay in front of them.

There it was again. The same carpet that clashed in his eyes almost causing him physical pain. Each time he saw it, his memory jerked into hundreds of images of its tastelessness.

'Just don't look at it,' said Rebecca. 'Come on, we'll go straight to the Duty Free lounge.' But it was in there too and she had to admit to its vulgarity.

'If only the British had some of the Italians' style.' Her words led them straight to Florence and for the first time Noel mustered enthusiasm. He was on a bridge overlooking the Arno, his shadow elongated by the rays of the sun casting its pale hues in the water.

The flight was called, they took their seats. The take-off was deliciously smooth.

She would not lie around and moan or sulk. Noel would be back in two weeks. It wasn't long and the next day was the party. That only gave her two weeks to practise. She plotted a strict routine, thinking again about running. Normally she hated the sport and commiserated over its victims, the friends of hers who'd been caught and become addicted. But it had advantages: it would be quick and provide some physical release.

She dressed in a track suit, t-shirt and trainers, pulling her hair back in a pony tail. The sporty image suited her although the idea to remain a voyeur was strong. 'I'll start with a couple of blocks along the river,' she thought, and with a small amount of confidence set off.

It was quite successful, although a little painful, gasping for air. At least it had seemed incongruous to pine with the pounding of her feet and the revolt by her muscles demanding attention.

The programme she planned to play at the party was forty-five minutes, with another few pieces, if she was asked to play more. Since it was an informal event she decided to split movements and play classics everyone would recognize. It was a compromise but she assessed the situation, concluding that the champagne would have taken its toll on the majority of her listeners by the time she played.

For three hours she practised, pausing as she thought of Noel's plane taking off, allowing herself to harbour on his talent, his large artisan hands that drew her out into their world. She made a peanut butter sandwich and listened to a recording of the Grovlez 'Sarabande et Allegro'.

Marcus phoned and talked her into seeing a film that evening, and committed himself to the daily running experiment. He seemed to survive on no sleep, which was the key, Briony thought, to success.

Most of the afternoon she devoted to the new music, enjoying the challenge, going over and over again the same few bars. First with the left hand and then the right, the reward being when she joined them together. It was a moody piece, at once sharp and exciting, then rhythmic and melodic, ending high on a crescendo. The more she played the more she liked it and became intrigued about the mystery clarinettist she had yet to meet. After the flute, the clarinet was her favourite wind instrument with its deep woody tones, mature mid-range and high octaves. She tried to hum its part but the range far exceeded her own.

By six o'clock she complimented herself on getting through the day with such ease, she multiplied it by thirteen and that seemed for ever. She criticized herself for resting hopes on something as unpredictable as a man. Sooner or later, while he was away, she knew she must come to a decision. She looked at her hands, the keys of the piano and thought of Marcus. She hoped she could decide with her head, and not her heart.

Too morose it made her, and insular, so she phoned Lizzie, whose flat was nearby and convinced her to meet at the local pub. She hadn't seen Lizzie for a long time, not since the weekend in the country. She remembered being possessed by Noel, by the stream, thoughts of him strong and vibrant flowing in unison with the water. Was it the same now, she wondered?

TWENTY-THREE

Once they left the airport, its cold, colourless walls housing pandemonium and groaning conveyor belts, they emerged into the diaphanous light that flooded over Tuscany, centring itself in golden prisms on the steeples and domes of Florence.

Noel fell under its spell weaving through the narrow streets clanging with bells, the sounds of a city at work and the odd shuffle from the slippered feet of the homeless. He cursed the cruelty, which made him think of Briony, loath for anything to take enjoyment away from Rebecca. She was proud and strong; he winced as he thought of the pain he must have caused her. He measured himself next to her and found deficiencies at each evaluation. He smiled at her and held her hand between his, hesitant, unsure but then her eyes accepted his change of heart.

They were staying in a small *pensione* in Via de' Malcontenti. They had discovered it before, a jewel of simplicity away from the crowds. It was mid-afternoon and the sun was starting its descent. They sat in the wisteria-terraced garden at one of the square white tables. The wine poured, Noel proposed a toast. Their conversation started to relax. They had, after all these years, so many safe subjects to take refuge in.

Their room was small and Noel was conscious of the space closing in, leaving no privacy. He felt his responsibilities tighter here than at home with the post of brown enveloped bills and the intrusion of the telephone. It was going to be hard phoning Briony. Already he missed the machine. The change of scene, the foreign atmosphere, shook him up. He used it to monitor his sanity.

They decided after lunch to walk through Florence to feel the streets and linger on the bridges. They passed the Uffizi, finding to their surprise it was still open. Here they separated for the first time. Rebecca, tired by the journey and the wine, was quite content to leave Noel and wander slowly back to the *pensione*.

He bobbed his head like a turkey, looking this way and that, quite bristled by the intrigue. He counted his change, hundreds of lire but he would need thousands, or maybe millions. He could do it near the Duomo and capture a chime. No, he thought, he'd practise first with the money and then when he'd found the best telephone booth he'd give her the chime.

'Buon giorno amore,' he slipped in another token, it was gobbling them up. The machine, it was the machine. Phoning from all this way and the damn machine answers. 'Sorry, machine' he said as the message finished and he was on. 'I'm standing on the edge of the Piazza della Signoria in front of the dramatic Palazzo Vecchio,' he said in his mimic of a news reporter. 'The sky is blue, and I am too without you. This is better than writing a diary. How are you?' he continued getting into the rhythm of dropping his tokens in. 'How are you little machine, feeling neglected no doubt. Well, it's that naughty mistress of yours. You make sure she gives you a light dusting from me. *Arrivederci*,' and he blew her an Italian kiss, which he caught in his hand and threw over the square.

'Buona sera,' said a passer-by and Noel tipped an imaginary hat in his direction.

Briony was growing restless with deceit. Noel had spilled out of the pocket he was confined to and the novelty of longing for him was growing thin. Not that it was imperfect when they were together. He just wasn't there enough.

She had never seen him angry, or shy, impatient, out of his depth, and felt a passion for hate, to look at him with something other than the loosely termed feelings of love. She wanted fire in his eyes, resolve, the fearlessness of risks, not some illicit rendezvous.

'Briony, did you hear?'

'I'm sorry Lizzie, you were telling me, Camille's auditioning for the Philharmonic?'

Slipping in and out of her life and his until she didn't know which was which. This harping always, for more. Lizzie was bringing her back to the time they were all training at the College, who was making headway who was not, who got married, who gave up. Lizzie was good herself but she'd taken a job at a hotel playing the same old love songs every night.

They arranged to meet at Marengo's for Briony's next gig. Lizzie hoped Briony would be less distracted then.

'Hello machine,' she said as she got home, hung up her coat and turned it on. 'Oh Noel' she forgave him all and wallowed in his voice, the deep baritone, with his northern chat and Italian accent. What she felt at the sound of his voice could not be a habit. She shivered as she imagined how she felt when he touched her. She longed for his hands on her and was then shy at her promiscuity. But she was not promiscuous. It would change things if she was: another man, having what Noel owned. But he didn't, couldn't, own her. They had talked, it was her ammunition to even it out, if she took a lover. He would understand, he said so. He would maybe understand, or tuck it away if she did, as long as it wasn't like them. They had that security that they were the only ones. Still she wanted to play with fate as it had played with her for so long now, stringing her along. Not tonight though, another time.

She went to the cinema less and less. At one time she saw every film which came out. Now it was all American, easy listening, lazy language, plots hanging onto a string of famous names. She held out hope for *The Revenge of Madame Bovary*, by a little known French director.

Marcus always arrived with a package, wine, a bunch of violets and tonight a delicacy: desert truffles. They didn't look appetizing these small, brown and wrinkly nuggets but he shaved them onto some foie gras and the taste was exquisite. Briony enjoyed the versatility of Marcus' character. He felt responsible for teaching her finer graces, a knowledge he had acquired from an exclusive education somewhere down the line. She felt privileged to share such invaluable information. She was amazed by his eclectic bank of curious learnings. She pinned him down for dinner next week, he'd let her off so many times by eating out. Noel was far from her thoughts until she went to turn the machine on. Her sympathies were with the machine, she almost felt like leaving it a saucer of milk and then thought better of her feeble mind.

They picked a night when summer warmth seduced other cinema-goers away. Side by side they felt each other's presence, the force of the film bringing them together as they shared the lives on the screen. They linked arms to leave, walking in silence with thoughts left by the film, prolonging the effect as long as possible. This time she called the tune, taking him to a hole-in-the-wall Vietnamese restaurant where the spices wrapped around their tastebuds and the waiters were proud of their compliments.

'Tomorrow there's a party. Will you come?'

She agreed.

At home she felt a dullness sweep over her as if some essential ingredient was missing. She looked around at the rows and rows of albums and tapes and hummed a few notes in her head. They came from nowhere. At first she thought it was from the film, something she'd heard but each time she added a few more or a new variation to the old, it sounded quite original. She played them through her head again and then went to the piano. It was late but she didn't care. She tried them in one key and then another. Right hand only, over and over until she had the tune. Hastily she wrote it down least, like so many late night ideas she might forget.

The next day she was up and out of the house.

'Briony, why are you always in a rush? Lateness is not a characteristic for a concert pianist. Let's start with the "Sarabande et Allegro",' said Natalie.

TWENTY-FOUR

The business with the telephone made Noel feel like a sleuth. Intrigue, together with his foreign surroundings, fuelled his sense of the macabre. He stopped at a café for an espresso and cognac and struck up a conversation with the waiter. His Italian was limited but with effective hand signals he made himself understood. What was life but a charade he said, which was interpreted in many ways by his colleagues at the bar, no one having understood what he meant. He had another round and left to a chorus of *'Ciao, Inglese.'*

Rebecca's feet were killing her. Vanity would be exchanged for comfort from now on. She soaked in a bath relieved that Noel was on a lead but feared that at any moment he would break loose and cause an uproar. She liked his unpredictability, aversion to conforming and originality. But she also disliked the same traits. She was looking forward to lying on the beach, soaking up the sun. If only England had better weather, or some weather. She refused to think of the approaching winter, each day grey, grey before and grey again.

Rebecca had already made friends with the lady on reception, Signora Guiliano. She had a portly stance, that flowed from within the layers of her black petticoats. Rebecca imagined she had borne many sons and that most of them were the waiters or porters in the *pensione*. Her hair was sharply tidied away in a tight bun that swirled around her head like a ripple of chocolate in vanilla ice-cream.

The last evening sun strained through the window, settling on the little writing desk in the corner of the room. It was a different light to home and the air seemed less poignant. What could they do tonight? A meal somewhere. She'd ask the Signora Guiliano but first she'd study the guide books and personal recommendations. The last time she and Noel had been out for dinner was that frigid time when he was acting most strangely. The memory haunted her. He wanted to make love but she, so unused to his affection, had felt cold, glacial in his arms. It was a half-hearted awkwardness. She blamed herself they were so different that way, Noel affectionate, constantly demanding attention and she restricted by inhibition. She would try to loosen up, maybe wine would help.

Noel dressed carefully as if clean clothes would give him a clean conscience. He noticed at once that his shirts were creased and he had left his trousers at home, except for a pair that were baggy, white and paint-stained. He took them off and called room service for an iron. The room seemed too small for the two of them. He was acutely aware of Rebecca, sitting at the writing desk looking through the guidebooks while he bungled through his toilette. All the uneasiness he associated with travel was there and he longed to be in Briony's flat closeted by the desire they shared. Rebecca and he moved in the room like carefully choreographed dancers. Years of living together had made them intuitive to each other's way of doing things. The iron arrived and Rebecca did not look up while he battled alternatively with the board and then his collar.

Downstairs the wisteria garden was lit by multi-coloured bulbs, the smell from the flowers swept over the tables, and now tomato sauce and melted cheese wafted in from the kitchen. At first they were tempted by its allure but Noel insisted they go further into Florence.

It was still warm enough for short sleeves and the shops were open to seduce money from tourists' wallets. The lights from the Ponte Vecchio reflected in the river like a sheet of mirror, while the water deflected voices carried from open air cafés. They walked towards the Medici Palace stopping for a drink in the Piazza del Duomo until they heard the sound of voices coming from a slit of a passageway. They followed the noise to some cast iron steps that opened onto an overgrown garden with a large sign 'LA DOLCE VITA'. Inside, it seemed, was a strictly Italian clientèle, which didn't take kindly to foreigners. Noel felt his clothing scrutinized. He could pay the bill and that, to him, was all that mattered. The gold of Rebecca's eye-shadow caught his eye and he looked at her in a filial way and thought that was the closeness they had come to. She was enchanted by the place, by the chance to have a husband again.

Afterwards they wandered back to the *pensione* hand in hand. The Duomo rang out midnight and the sound of the bells reminded Noel of his promise to Briony. Rebecca's hand, warm in his, gave out her forgiveness. Noel squeezed it dishonestly and felt Rebecca cling on with expectation. In the room he tried not to watch her undress, hoping she would fall asleep but he could feel her watching him, waiting.

He slipped between the covers, keeping to his side of the bed. Rebecca reached out to him, leaving him no choice. They had two weeks together, he would have to tell her, but not now. She was kissing him but his lips felt dead on hers. She pulled him closer towards her and he tried to masquerade his weak affection. He couldn't stop her now, he owed her this at least, to make love to his wife.

That night Briony couldn't sleep. She tossed and overheated under the duvet, waking with tiredness to exorcize the fearful stories which wrecked her sleep. Then she would fall back in a haze trying to calm herself with a safe fantasy, floating, illusory, something intangible but her heart would fight back, sometimes beating so hard the feel of it frightened her. It was all hyperbole in the night where shadows danced and then disappeared, time would tick by and then each minute would never end. What was it that filled her mind with troubled thoughts? But she was never awake enough to find out and the images drifted with her in and out of sleep all night.

She was sure when she finally woke that she'd had a bad dream, that was all, until she felt the niggling after effects of her restlessness. It was probably MSG in the Vietnamese food. She was perfectly all right. Tonight she would sleep, deep and sound.

As she drew the curtain the light shone upon each speck of dust, highlighting it like a spotlight. She must do something about the flat, it was a mess. In this light, even the piano had a thin layer of dust. Most of it came from the street, no matter how much she cleaned, which wasn't often, the dust would still collect like a colony of ants. It would take all day trying to make the place look good for her dinner with Marcus tonight.

The doorbell rang and it was him, exposing fine muscular legs which she saw for the first time. The running: she'd forgotten.

'Just a minute Marcus, I'll be right there.'

The shower beat down on her disappointment. She missed Noel bitterly. He was wrapped up like a mummy in all his good points and she was blind to anything else. In his absence he was again the man who had evoked all her sensitivities. But her affections needed to be stoked, she needed his attentions.

She was glad of her piano lesson today. Otherwise she might stay in, just in case he phoned. She went through the pieces she would be working on, limbering up first with scales, arpeggios and a few studies.

Natalie was a petite woman whose apparently fragile size gave no hint of her real strength. This little woman with close-cropped hazelnut-coloured hair could virtually move a piano by herself. Her deportment was impeccable and she walked with her feet turned slightly outward which drew attention to her tiny stockinged feet in sensible good quality shoes. She was Parisian, married to an Englishman, but her accent never changed no matter how many years went by.

'Briony, Good Morning,' she always emphasized the 'ning'.

'Hello Natalie, I love that Grovlez piece, I've been practising it all weekend.'

'That is good, because I want you and Calum to start practising together. You will like him, Calum. He is technically very good, but he has a certain feeling that I think will mix well with the way you play. So come on, show me what you have learned.'

Natalie was a perfectionist and there were times when Briony couldn't measure up to her standards. They had fought like snarling dogs, a bad day, tiredness, feelings of low self-worth all contributing, but in the end all it did was tighten the bond between them.

'No, no, no! Too fast.'

Natalie was off, but today Briony wanted to work. She wanted her hands and mind to sweat with toil which was needed to get the music right.

The pasta was performing acrobatics in his stomach. As if it wasn't enough to eat the stuff once, thought Noel as he lay on his back trying to divorce himself from the activity within him.

Normally he put it down to paranoia. These days everything was health. There were too many fatal diseases about that clashed with today's concept of immortality. Everywhere you went there were health shops and pills for everything, fat legs, sleepless nights, nerves, stress, tension. But this, the solo performance by the pasta in his stomach was not in his imagination. Now it was the big dipper, four ravioli climbing into a car which was to take them to the top. He couldn't bear it, he was going to have to get up. Where could he go, he had too much pride to go and spill his guts in the tiny bathroom approximately two feet away from where Rebecca was sleeping. If he was going to retch it was not in this room. With that decision he put on his moccasins and the towelling dressing gown he'd brought for the beach and set off down the corridor to find a communal bathroom.

Once he was up he felt much better and then it hit him. The carload of ravioli on the big dipper had become a whole train and they had reached the top. Seized by panic Noel tried a door, it was locked, he turned and like a vision saw the beckoning bowl of a lavatory two rooms up. The ravioli paused just long enough for Noel to get his head down.

He was weak but the circus was over. He heard footsteps on the stairs and realized the door was still wide open. He slammed it shut and turned the tap on, splashing his face with cold water and relieving his dry throat. His legs were shaky, but he felt better. He tiptoed back along the passageway and eased his way past the squeak of the door into his bedroom. Rebecca hadn't stirred. He slipped in between the sheets and felt himself sinking down, down into comfort, oblivion.

TWENTY-FIVE

The noise outside crescendoed with the breaking day. There were clunks from unloading delivery vans, a buzzing of voices shouting instructions, dustmen roughly heaving bins, fresh bread scenting the air, brakes squeaking, engines choking, the sounds of a city waking up.

It was most unusual for Noel to sleep through such a racket, but he was oblivious to the early morning thrill of his new surroundings. Rebecca, who had followed the progress of the day through a light doze, dressed quietly and, not wanting to wake him, left a note and went downstairs.

Waking alone was unusual for Noel. At first he spread himself out like a windmill luxuriating in the space. Rebecca's note swept into the air by his shuffling, spiralled in flight on its way to the floor. His first thought on reading it reeked of conspiracy. The bill, the telephone calls would be on it. What difference would it make, he paid it anyway and he reached for the telephone with confident familiarity. He needed to talk to her, feel they were not so far apart, but instead their distance was exaggerated by the woolly line, the time it took to connect. I hope it isn't Bonzo who answers he thought.

'Hello machine, where's your mistress? This is the second time I've phoned. I know you may want to hear from me but you've got to stop sending Briony out when you know I'll phone.

'I'm in this huge bed. It must be lovely for you, I mean Briony, stretching out, wiggling your toes. So much room. I was so sick last night. Terrible night I had.'

As he spoke he decided he would spend his time sketching places in Florence, people there that he could use in his drawings, he became quite enamoured of the idea and impatient to get out to his arena of research, as he called it.

'I'll try to reach you later, my love. Enjoy yourself, honestly.'

He was losing weight and his exercise the night before accentuated this. His belt tightened another notch, gathering the now slack material in folds around his bottom.

Rebecca was having breakfast in the garden. 'Hello Noel, you were flat out this morning, I thought you probably needed the rest.'

'That tuna ravioli must have had something dicey in it, I was up half the night trying to keep it down. What have we got here?'

He fingered some dry biscottes and ordered a cappuccino.

'Noel, I've been offered another job on a new film. It's a lot of work but I think I'd like to do it. You're away so much of the time or in your studio working and I am on my own too much. I think it would do me good now Tammy's got much more of her own life.'

He knew it. He'd known that she was up to something and was aware they had been skirting about the issue. Perhaps this was it. And then it struck him. Perhaps she had a lover. The indignity swept through him like a clap of thunder, causing him to start with the shock. How could she look at him with lying eyes? He fell into a response that neither acknowledged or continued the conversation. Wasn't she concerned that he had spent half the night throwing up?

It would be easy for her to have a liaison with someone. He'd been blind, so busy with Briony. What irony, that Rebecca might be up to such covert operations. He could not accuse her of his suspicions. Perhaps it would be best for them both to go with new lovers.

Rebecca took Noel's silence for inner scheming. He was thinking how much freer he would be, how much more available for a mistress, if he had one. Although Rebecca had been temporarily consoled by Noel's strange conversation with the machine she had later thought that someone would receive his soliloquy. It could only be someone he knew intimately, the sort of closeness associated with lovers.

She felt they were making ground. The meal last night in the idyllic restaurant. They'd made love. Oh dear, so Noel had been sick. She thought he made the wrong choice but sometimes he could be so touchy, she hadn't wanted to bring it up. There were still rumblings of severed lines in their conversation.

Neither of them spoke until the silence, which at first was unsettling, drifted into the sort of space which was quite acceptable to a couple who had known each other a long time. Many thoughts, accusations and assumptions had crossed both their minds and after brief evaluation they decided to avoid confrontation. The waiter appeared with Noel's coffee, they pruned the bulk of their preoccupation and planned the day to make the best use of their time.

Noel agreed briefly to go shopping. The Italian cut generally complimented his figure and he could do with a new pair of trousers having left his old ones at home. After lunch they would go their separate ways. Noel would take his sketch book and go to the Galleria dell'Accademia while Rebecca looked for a handbag and cased the shops on the Ponte Vecchio. Everyone knows you don't buy anything there, she said, but she wanted to look in the tiny shops which hang from the bridge.

Strangely enough the equality of their cheating, the cards being turned on Noel, gave him a new sense of respect for Rebecca. He saw her again as a challenge, someone to be wooed, chased and courted, not taken for granted the way he had for many years. His eyes danced with innuendo and when he looked at her his gestures became self-conscious instead of governed by habit.

The day was perfect. He breathed in the air and filled his senses with the beauty of Florence. It was not hard to imagine the streets as they might have been hundreds of years before, to see the Medicis and the Grand Dukes of Tuscany in conference or preparing for a ball in the buildings he passed. He felt so awake, fresh, light and trouble-free inside, a good feeling after the months of twisted thoughts and crippled loyalties. How he would love to show all this to Briony. He saw how clearly her face would light up, she was always so enthusiastic, never cynical or worn down the way he sometimes felt.

Rebecca went into a shop while he waited outside a café and sketched an old man with a cigarette hanging on his lower lip, his eyes ringed by many years, his long labourer's hands cupped over a brandy. Their eyes met as he watched Noel invade his privacy. He looked as if he would get up and then something he saw changed his mind and his eyes dropped their defence and filled with compassion. Noel finished and came up to him.

'Ancora?'

He pointed to the brandy. The man waved him to sit. Noel showed him the sketch and he twitched a sign of recognition, taking in his years and the character Noel had put on paper. He wanted to see more and Noel showed him his book. He took pleasure in seeing a whole life unfold from a single drawing. The brandy came and Noel paid. Rebecca came out of the shop and started to look for him.

Noel signalled he must go, and got up. The old man lifted his arm to acknowledge it all.

TWENTY-SIX

The pupil after Briony was late. Like a galley slave on a Viking's ship she had worked and worked to Natalie's command and the two of them were quite exhausted when time was up. Later that week Calum McGuire would be there and they'd have their first practice together.

She was playing at the hotel tonight and then it was Marcus' party. She decided to buy the food for tomorrow night and then try to get an hour's sleep, otherwise she'd never last the pace.

Before she turned the key she knew Noel would have phoned. Once she didn't mind when she missed his calls, knowing he would phone back. Now it grated on her nerves, she was so unattainable. She was sure he would reach her today, hours remained before she went out again.

Marcus had seen the doubt as he watched her melancholy. There was a unique reaction between the two, but Briony was losing interest or the will for staying power. Marcus had no doubt that it would only be a matter of time before Noel realized he might lose her. Could he reach her by then? Marcus knew she had never thought of him in that way, but there had been moments, which he was sure would increase now that Noel was away. He could not give her what Noel did, this uncanny sense of communicating on their own plane, he didn't know how to put it, but he'd seen them with looks, hold a conversation. Did he want to gamble with his heart this way? If he was to be truthful, she had always fascinated him, without knowing why, he liked the way nothing ever fell into habit, nothing was predictable.

Noel did not phone that day and it knocked him down a notch in her opinion. She had reached the point where she couldn't long for him any harder without it shredding her life into pieces she would be unable to put back together again. Always it seemed she was pivoting round the circumference while he pulled her strings like a puppet.

Tonight she would be a chameleon. First she would wear her hair straight and brushed until it shone while she played to the diners at the Godsbury Hotel and then when it was over she would douse it in extra-hold gel and squeeze herself into the black stretch jumpsuit. She sensed it was a night that would not be disguised behind luxury. When she was ready she left the flat without turning on the answering machine.

The scratch of her high-heeled shoes on the pavement resonated in her ears, clashing with the pound of indecision until she could bear it no longer. Damn him, she thought as she retraced her steps and ran up the stairs. The phone was ringing, she picked it up, it was him.

She had not said a word and still he was talking, painting with his words a picture for her to share. When he did at last stop she said, 'Perhaps you will take me there one day.'

And he answered: 'You know that's impossible.'

Then he ran out of money and was gone.

What was she to do? Wait while he went to the nearest café to get telephone tokens? Perhaps his circumstances would prevent him phoning back immediately and she would be waiting for nothing. He knew she was playing at the hotel but would he remember, there in Florence, when his mind was obviously on other things?

She went to put on the machine but for some reason it would not rewind the outgoing message. The only way she could think of getting it to work was by recording another message. 'I've gone to play a gig,' she said, 'I'll be back late but you can ring me in the morning.' The machine sat back on its spools and waited for Noel to ring.

Noel was beginning to know the telephone booths of Florence quite intimately. At first he'd had a little trouble sorting out his change. There was something about this new-found knowledge that whisked him off the tourist track into a realm equating him with the locals. At first he'd looked a fool asking in phrase book Italian how to use the thing, now he waltzed in there, hunched over the phone and went about the business of dialling as if he'd lived there all his life.

He had enough time to realize the misunderstanding. It was an unusual thing for Briony to say. Until now she had never made a demand, never expected what was due naturally to a woman who had given herself to a man. Briony had understood all along that he was not in control of his life. He must reassure her, she could not know that she was always with him in ways far beyond logicalities such as time or distance. Yes, he must tell her that now, straight away, and with the impending excitement of hearing her voice his fingers had stuck to the dials in his rush to be connected and he had to start dialling again.

She came home steeped in wine and self-indulgence. Her lack of shame pointed the blame at Noel. Yet she knew the source of her unhappiness was through her weakness of loving him. She longed at once to be free of him and still to have him. It was a desperation and a desire, the contradiction between giving up everything and at the same time wanting more than she had. Again she weighed up the disadvantages and yet, insurmountable as they seemed, it was something far beyond logic that drew her to him. She resolved to stop loving him and yet she wanted him more. No, his life was not compatible with hers. They were dreams that met together, but as a life they would continually disappoint each other: too much hope, expectation. But there was always that lingering thought, that one gamble, that perhaps – a tiny perhaps – it would be worth it. But the weight of his life on hers? Him giving everything up. If it was everything, a wife, a child, a home, was it everything? To her it didn't seem so but to him, he must have thought so once.

It was his choice. It always would be, because he had everything. It seemed so one-sided but it was not, she was really the one who had everything, because she had freedom. Wasn't that what he was giving up? To get what she already had? But she was ready to share it with him. Share without commitment because she was already used to that.

The intoxication of that night, the party, rolled her up like a roaring wave. As the wave had grown with momentum she was spun within it, to be thrown, dazed, back, eventually, to her familiar surroundings.

It all began at the hotel. Everyone must have been on holiday because the restaurant was empty. A few couples and three solitary diners were dotted about the room where she played. The waiters, with nothing to do, had whisked them through their meals before an ambience set in. Without an atmosphere, however temporary, of smooth velvety opulence, the notes she played seemed to have no destination, and they wafted without direction or a thrill of seduction, for there was no one in the room to romance with her playing. The diners came and went as in a railway waiting room. She could have been a piece of litter swept in by the wind as the door opened and out again by a draught.

When Marcus came into the hushed room she longed for the medicine Alice in Wonderland had taken to make herself small. Although she had played on and off for three hours her hands were still cold.

There was a room in the basement, next to the kitchen, which she used to change. Marcus bought a bottle of champagne from a waiter and when she finished playing they went downstairs to the tiny room with no windows, decorated by a cracked mirror and wall of grey paint-chipped lockers. It smelt of musk and old shoes.

Marcus looked like a punk, evil in his blackness. His hair, which was black and long in front, had been slicked and combed over his forehead where it hung in groups of strands over his searching black eyes. Normally they were dark blue. He wore tight black trousers hugging his legs and dissolving into pointed black boots. His black polo neck hung loose by comparison.

The sleaziness of the room was bringing her back to life: the dustballs which lined the floor skirting, the ripped wallpaper in the corners, the postcards the waiters stuck on their locker doors, and, in the midst, Marcus drinking champagne the same way he did when they were at Martino's. She couldn't wait to change, get out of this 'frock': she thought of the perfectly nice, short-sleeved fitted-waist, full-skirted dress she was wearing. 'Nice' – Noel hated that word.

Marcus was sitting like a cat ready to pounce, lying comfortably on one of its lives. She pulled on the stretch fabric feeling it cling to her like another layer of skin. There wasn't a ripple of skin that could hide behind a tuck or a gather. She took a thick, glob of gel, moulding it in her hands and squelched it into her hair. She exaggerated her eyes with eyeliner, shaping them like almonds, and combing her lashes with mascara. Her high cheekbones she sharpened with rouge, pink and melon blending them into the pale colour of her skin without looking cadaverous. Bright red was too vital for her fine features so she flooded her lips with a pink which balanced her eyes and shadow-drenched cheeks.

He was busy with a razor blade making neat lines of cocaine. She never wanted to know how involved Marcus was, better that they left that area hazy. She accepted tonight and soon their conversation raced through narrow corridors up the stairs, around the bend, past crannies and cobwebs of old ideas.

They went by taxi to a huge warehouse block, south of the river where stray couples drifted through the dark and seemed to enter the building as shadows.

The party was to celebrate Mungo and the Sextettes' first album. Marcus had negotiated the deal and the album had gone to be pressed. Briony liked Mungo although she had only met him once. He was a great showman, but not an extrovert by nature. The Sextettes were essentially a grass roots jazz band which the record company had tried to glitter up a bit. Revolution plc, the record company, had backed the right bands and made enough money to build four fully equipped recording studios. The party was held in an open plan warehouse that used to house the whole operation.

There was a bouncer on the door who okayed their entrance with a sly nod. It was nearly midnight and the place was beginning to fill. Thank god she hadn't worn a coat at a party like this. Dave Pritchard the PR man threw an arm around Marcus and motioned approval at Briony. He was pleased by the turn-out: most of his repertoire of socialites, models and celebrities had shown up. Mungo and the band's friends were quite a different set and they could be singled out by their lack of ostentation. Mungo himself was wearing a red suede jacket with a fringe down both arms, and across the back he had a cowboy hat from which he had hung a number of corks coated in glue and then dipped in gold and silver sequins. His wine glass looked tiny in his huge hand, so did the delicate party snacks which balanced precariously in the other.

'It'll be good in a couple of hours when all the icing's gone,' said Mungo. 'We're going to play later but Dave's got to do his bit, get a few hacks to write a snippet or two in the papers. Once he's got his publicity quota I reckon it will be a wild time.'

'Hello, it's Briony, isn't it? An unusual name. You play with the Main Street Cavaliers sometimes, don't you? I don't know if you're into the same stuff as us but we're going to have a jam session later on and there's a Yamaha just perched on the stage. Have a word with Duke.'

She'd love to play. She knew exactly what they played because she'd been to see them at least a dozen times. The guys at Marengo's played four songs from their repertoire. Mungo was one of the best sax players on the circuit, what a privilege to play with them.

If only Noel could be here. She wondered what he'd think of the party, the people, this weird bunch in the prime of their idealism. He was her age in the sixties when drugs and love were commonplace – sex 'n drugs and rock and roll. It wasn't like that now in the age of caution. Most of her friends had calmed down, there were always a few who still smoked and the breed of city slickers who would do the odd pick-me-up, but for the most part people didn't even smoke cigarettes or drink caffeine.

The music was being piped in through a quadraphonic system and pumped through conversations, but it had to be loud to fill the room. She met a couple of people she knew and was talking to a friend of Duke's when Marcus retrieved her. Marcus didn't leave her alone much, but she didn't mind. She would have been lost without his introductions into the cliques.

Duke came up and said they were about to play. Many people were dancing and the stage was starting to fill as musicians set up their microphones and started tuning their instruments. They decided on 'Lazy Mandy', one of Briony's favourite songs that Mungo had written, she'd join them after a few songs.

It was one of those rare evenings when everything melds perfectly. The euphoria from the band, the high of finishing the album and now relaxing was infectious. The room was less crowded and the hard core, the real friends of the band, was left. They played without the restrictions a club or clientèle demand, improvising. At one point they had an extra six saxophone players, and four trumpets. Elsa Martingayle sang two throaty numbers. She wasn't in London much now that she was a headliner. Briony was too excited to be nervous. For the musicians here was a rare chance to play as they felt, with no quota of sets to fill. She loved 'Lazy Mandy', so did Mungo, and the two of them went off on a tangent after the last chorus. It was the same feeling she had when she was with Noel.

TWENTY-SEVEN

Noel took refuge amongst the stony figures of the four slaves and David in the Galleria dell'Accademia. When he'd heard the machine only a few minutes after his money had run out, he was exasperated. How could she be so unkind? Here he was in Florence trying to phone her from a call box. It was not easy, he had to be careful choosing his moments. He pounded at her thoughtlessness never thinking of what she had said: that she was late, she'd have to leave. The audacity of it overwhelmed him.

He'd grown used to reaching her at his convenience. They never talked about her, what it was like to be the one who waited. It was uncanny, how his nose was out of joint and yet he did not consider that she might have commitments.

The cold marble doused his dilemma, and he took out his book and began to sketch, letting his mood influence the tone of his drawing. Occasionally he would lose his concentration and play with the idea of not phoning her but soon he would be wanting her again. In the late afternoon he went back to the *pensione* and phoned the machine, aware that the machine was protecting her: it would deliver the message. How easily it switches its allegiance, he thought. Although the machine was hers, he was the one that confided in it, he was the one who had given it the respect of feeling.

He left the *pensione* shortly before he knew Rebecca would return. Noel wanted more time on his own.

*

Rebecca had survived the embarrassment of Noel's assault on a pair of baggy, fawn, Georgio Armani trousers with immense refinement. She'd known they would look hopeless on him, he was too stocky to carry off the bulk of pleats below the front waistband. He'd squeezed on a size too small, not realizing how loose they should be and held up his jacket to see them in the mirror. One of his pens' caps must have come off, because ink had seeped through and had just enough time to soil the ill-fated Armanis. The shop assistant had seen immediately – the stain was large and black – and had insisted on unzipping them while Noel reacted to protect his modesty. Once they were off he was left standing in the front of the shop wearing an obscene pair of boxer shorts, a pair Rebecca had never seen before. Instead of putting his trousers on Noel became profuse with apologies, probably afraid he would have to pay for the trousers. Rebecca had gone up to him and said: 'Here, Noel put these on at once,' and then she tried to make herself invisible.

The event, which they didn't have to pay for, curtailed Noel's enthusiasm for shopping and they decided to part and pursue their own interests, on their own.

Noel was not the sort of man to buy a handbag with, so in a way Rebecca didn't mind that he'd gone off to sketch some of Michelangelo's work. The bottom-pinching stereotypes she feared from her younger days appeared to have grown up, or was it her age, she wondered. The only acknowledgement she received from this once hot-blooded race was the occasional 'bella' as she walked down the streets.

She began around Piazza San Giovanni where she fell upon a nest of shops whose windows glinted chocolate-smooth leather, butterscotch gloves and endless possibilities. She indulged herself buying an ochre tailored suit in one shop and finding the mink-coloured handbag she had been looking for in another. The suit was wrapped in mountains of unwrinkled tissue paper and folded into a thin, rectangular box, made with a handle of twisted candy-coloured string. Such shopping was a cherished treat so unlike the battleground of Oxford Street.

A small café down a side street sent a gust of freshly percolated coffee beans, which guided her straight to its lair. There she savoured every sip, resting her feet before heading off again towards the Duomo.

That night they dined in the wisteria garden of the *pensione*. The fresh air, the shopping and accumulative hours in a museum had tired them out. Noel had moderated the explicit affair Rebecca was having in his imagination. Tomorrow they would rent the car and stay in a small hotel on the way to the coast. He would have liked more time in Florence, but it was too complicated to change the arrangements. Their appreciation of the warmth, the perfect late summer night, the smell of the wisteria, taste of Chianti alongside the three-course meal, removed all nuances. They were, after all, longtime friends.

At seven o'clock Noel crept out of the room to find a telephone. He toyed for a moment with consideration, it was only six o'clock in London, but his longing to talk to her, no matter how sleepy she might be, overruled. When the machine answered, he slunk into a small ball feeling like a rag doll discarded on a nursery floor.

Noel hadn't missed her by long. Her feet dragged wearily up the steps, followed by the heavy tread of Marcus, shortly after he phoned. She still heard the applause and music ringing as a dull thud. Somehow, after such exultation under the spotlight, to be thrown back onto the steps leading to her flat seemed quite deflating. Marcus tried to effuse some vivacity, which fell quite flat. Then the tiredness that infiltrated every pore led her to his arms. Within the distortion of the remaining night she imagined herself with Noel, alone, far away. She opened her eyes with her head on Marcus' shoulder which caught the flashing light of the answering machine. It would never let her forget him. She moved away from Marcus, who watched his chance disintegrate. He was wise enough to leave.

They must, at the same time, have wanted each other equally. He, stooped in the small Italian *pensione,* and she in languor, both needing each other for sustenance. But instead they cursed each other's absence, Noel becoming filled with doubt: it was, after all, so early in the morning that he assumed she had not come home, and she was too tired to replay his message. No words on a tape could offer consolation. She at least had sleep coming to refresh her, Noel had breakfast with Rebecca.

For a while she thought she had conquered him, by having the night to herself, a few hours here and there during the day. He was a parasite clinging to parts of her life that were her own. With the dying end of such thoughts she went to bed, conscious of the machine, knowing even in her sleep he was trying to reach her.

Breakfast on the sun-filled patio lost its charm. Sensing a new distance, Rebecca tried to bridge it, letting their many years together bind them against the *pensione,* their fellow diners, the transitory familiarity of the waiters. He was content to fall into her chatter, to relish their last hours in the city. They had left their day-to-day domestic details behind by now, falling onto safe ground, a more general conversation cloaked with occasional suspicion. Rebecca knew time and heat were not the solution. 'Noel,' she whispered to herself. 'Is there someone else?'

A long time later, Briony opened her eyes and stretched liked a tiger baked in the sun. She felt the confidence given by a good night's sleep and tunnelled again into her duvet. It all came back to her in that ball of warmth under the covers: the band, how euphoric she had felt playing in that room filled with smoke and appreciation. Then Noel, how desperately she had wanted him to see and hear, but it would never be possible and that thought was as bitter as the wine she had drunk. Today in the lateness of the morning it did not seem the same at all and she looked to the machine for reassurance.

The hotel had booked her every night except Sunday for two weeks instead of the usual three nights a week. Curious, she thought, because the place was barely occupied. With three nights she could manage to keep a day schedule but the extra nights meant the nocturnal pattern would take over again. The distractions and demands on her time could only help take Noel out of the foreground.

She went to the fridge and found it full of polystyrene pots and packages from the deli counter which she'd bought for dinner that night. The therapeutic swirl she felt from the idea of cooking drenched her in momentary domestic bliss. The kettle boiled and she made a coffee. Then with the heat through the cup warming her hands she scooped up the courage to face the machine. She knew there were two messages from him because she could never help herself from looking at it, knowing its beady eye would always catch hers.

In a frenzy the machine responded to her flick of its switch; the sprockets chuckled with its whirls as the tape rewound faster and faster, then click, clunk, he was on.

She thought he was going to moan, although he never did directly. Neither of them did, it was in the silent pact that their love transcended moans, whines, or discontent. She was sure there would be a tone underneath it all asking, 'Why were you not there?' But there wasn't.

'I miss you Briony. More than I ever thought I could. I am growing so very tired of juggling within the lives of others, of hurting you, Rebecca, Tammy, the dog.' And she laughed because he didn't have a dog. His words were taking so long; they were going to say he would give everything up for her, she knew it already, but it took a long time to say it.

To think that she had not even listened to this message, that she had left it festering on the tape, filled her with guilt so bad she wanted to feel a physical pain, a cramping of her stomach at the very least to compensate the awfulness of what she had done. And then it fell on her with the weight and drama of a biblical revelation: did she really want what she had longed for all this time? Noel with her, here, in this flat, the two of them together. She eased herself into such thoughts gently, first with pampering, the snugness of waking next to him, the two of them having their coffee in the morning, the way she was now. Then the things which would change. Had she ever thought before, no she honestly could say she had never thought what it would be like. She had only wanted it so much that her life revolved around this lurking possibility. It always lurked and it was always possible, so the sheer suggestion of the thought becoming real, well, she had never let herself think of that. She loved him and that was what she wanted, wasn't it? It was still only a possibility, even though he had said it, he hadn't told her, he'd told the machine. She could hardly count that as Noel having told her. But never before had he hinted, had he said those words.

That was one of the things she liked. Just when she was so sure she was in control, the way she had been sure he was going to say something about her being out, he had turned her insides out, making them somersault. She turned the machine on and listened again to what he said. This time she let it run and there was another message.

Oh God! He had phoned this morning, before she got home. He had phoned to tell her everything and she had gone out on purpose knowing he would phone. Then he phoned again to wake her up and she had not been home. Phone him, reach him, track him down. She remembered the street, Via De'Malcontenti she couldn't forget that, the *pensione*, what was the name? He'd told her, think, she scrunched up her forehead squeezing it for information. She couldn't remember. Yes she could, it was there, it didn't have the word *pensione* in it, there was, something like, yes, that was it casa, house, casa di something. The river, Arno, that was it Casa D'Arno. International information, they made her wait, they didn't have the number but she knew they must. She never did this but this time she asked for a supervisor who yawned at her sense of urgency. Please help, she said under her breath and the silence ticked on. She got the number, the code, the dial tone and then she thought about Rebecca.

It was hard to dislike someone you had never met, someone whose fault was the same as yours. She reflected Noel's choices, she was an integral part of what Noel had thought he needed. Briony could only see hate coming from Rebecca towards her. Why not: through the selfless act of loving Noel she was destroying other people's lives. But it didn't seem like that because she didn't know these lives, she didn't know the other context.

'*Buon giorno*, Casa D'Arno.'

'Can I speak to one of your guests – Mr Noel Kenilmore?'

'No I am sorry, Mr and Mrs Kenilmore have checked out already.'

'Thank you,' she said.

She didn't know where he was, where he was going or staying. He was about as far from her as he could be.

Rebecca circled her spoon around the edge of her cup gathering a mouthful of foam from her cappuccino. She never did that. Yesterday, feeling provocative, she had bought silk stockings, so soft they slinked through her fingers on the way to the cash desk. Across the piazza where she was sitting a bird pecked at a stray pastry flake, grabbing a tiny piece in its beak and shaking the rest free. Was it the sorcery of Florence or a light dusting of resignation which had set her mind at rest?

She thought about her kitchen at home, remembering the sky as it was all the times she stared out of the window. She was tired then, feeling her life change around her while she watched. In a protective way she felt sorry for Noel, watching him frown and crunch up his face as if the thoughts were stacking in his mind and his filing capacity was full. Could she really be so objective, prepared to accept what seemed inevitable? Or did she think he would not know what to do with freedom and indulge him in an experimental fling and then ask to come home?

To think of everything she had worked for, falling, crashing down. Now she knew, it wasn't the life, the things, the securities, it was time, the years she had invested which could never be replaced. All the things she had resigned herself to never having again, she wanted, if she was to be without Noel. Tammy would be all right: children always survive, swaddled by resilience. A few fractures get etched on their memories. She would take a new wrinkle, weight loss, change of heart, all would eventually fade, leaving a scar that would join the others collected through the years.

The bird, tired of its game, flew off, up into the sky, over the city, it was soon a speck, and then nothing. She sighed. She was near the Giardino di Boboli and the Pitti Palace and set off in that direction.

Noel drifted around the gallery, finding the dampness of the cold stone walls reassuring. It seemed so obvious now, what he should do. What if he was too late? Where was she? Walking amongst the paintings, which gave him new aspirations and resolve towards his own work, he wondered why it had taken him so long to see things clearly. Perhaps it was Florence, the distance from home giving him a fresh perspective. Never had he wanted to see her so much, to show her everything here, knowing how intensely excited she would be. There was no conflict any more between the love of his work and his love for her. Now both loves had to be his life. Even as he looked at the paintings he felt it was not the same enjoyment as it would be if she was there.

When he left the Uffizi he felt tired and determined. How did he get talked into going to the Riviera, what did he want with a beach? The raw, pink, bubbling bellies of white holidaymakers filled him with loathing; he wanted quiet, away from the crowd, ideally away from himself.

Noel saw his raincoat in the simple oak armoire in his room at the *pensione*. His former room now, because Rebecca and he had checked out in the morning and left their luggage with the concierge. He had been reminded of it by a man in the street who was hosing down a scruffy wire-haired terrier. The running water in the gutter triggered his memory.

Signora Guiliano was proud to announce that room service had found the raincoat and produced it from behind the desk.

'There was a telephone call for you this afternoon, Signor Kenilmore. I think from England.'

'Did she leave a message?' said Noel.

'No, I am sorry, I said you had checked out.'

'Can I use the telephone please?'

'Yes, certainly. If you give me the number I will try it for you.'

She showed Noel to a small booth near the *pensione* entrance where he waited impatiently.

The line was busy. Yes try again, he said, and as he went back to the booth Rebecca walked in the front door.

'Your husband is making a telephone call,' Signora Guiliano kindly informed her.

'Hello Noel, who are you phoning?'

'Tammy,' he dribbled, 'I thought I'd give her a ring before we left.'

'That's a good idea, but she'll still be at school.'

'Oh yes, how silly of me, I forgot about the time difference.'

'Signor the number is ringing, shall I put your call through?'

'No thank you,' said Noel. 'I've just remembered, my daughter won't be home from school yet – you can cancel the call.'

She knows, thought Noel, that it was not my daughter. And Briony knew too that it was Noel who was phoning, because she'd heard the tone of long distance before she hung up.

*

Rebecca had convinced the rental company to deliver the car to the *pensione*, although she harboured doubts about it arriving on time. They were to drive north of Florence, find a hotel to stay in and the next day take a scenic route to the coast and follow it to Santa Margherita. She had got back to the *pensione* early because the Pitti Palace was closed. With time so precious she had been bitterly disappointed but as she walked back along the now familiar route, her frustration began to disperse. They had been lucky, she reasoned, not to have found more museums closed.

Noel liked to drive, and the thundering of small Italian cars circling the streets of Florence did not disturb him. Rebecca navigated but found it hard to find the street names and match them up before they seemed to be somewhere quite different. They skirted the city and headed off towards Pistoia, turning off into the dusk towards a town with an unpronounceable name.

TWENTY-EIGHT

It was a long time since Briony had spoken to Noel. She felt as if an umbilical cord had been cut, and resented him for being the one with the scissors.

The day, which started late, raced by giving her no satisfaction of having achieved anything at all. She looked at the machine with a conspiratorial glance, it was the only one who had communicated with them both. If only she didn't have to go out, he was bound to phone then.

Trying with difficulty to resign herself to Noel's inaccessibility she went to practise. She was meeting Calum later to put together the Grovlez piece. At least her fingers were fluid, as if all her aggravation and frustrations were pouring like electricity from a cable through her hands and the current sprinkling onto the keys and sparking.

There was a certain warmth between the two of them from the first time they touched hands to the way their eyes met, professionally, through the music. Calum was tall and thin, far too thin, not manly at all, but his hands were strong, with long sturdy fingers and perfect nails. She at once thought he needed to be fed up a bit, take some exercise. He was handsome too, without the innocent sensitivity many of the musicians she'd played with evinced.

Natalie was like a puffed-up robin strutting about with the confidence of her matchmaking success. From her old wooden filing cabinets she brought out a repertoire of music for clarinet and piano. Play this, now try that one. She saved the Grovlez for last and by the time they played it they had fallen into an understanding, a careful timing and both sensed the potential.

'Next week, the same time,' said Natalie showing them out with a shopping list of sheet music.

'I enjoyed playing with you,' said Calum. 'Do you want to have a practice before we meet with Natalie?'

'Yes, after I've had a chance to do some of this homework. Do you have a piano?'

'No, it would probably be easier if I came to you.'

'All right then, give me your number and we will talk.'

'Do you want to go for a coffee?'

'No thanks,' said Briony. Maybe next time. 'I'm playing at the Godsbury Hotel tonight and I haven't got time. Which way are you going?' They were going in opposite directions so they said goodbye and both looked over their shoulders as if to get one more glance of each other as they walked off.

Marcus had just had a bath, she could tell. She could smell the aroma of scented bath water and feel the effect of oil which had soaked in and softened his skin. His clean cheeks patted against hers with the closeness of a recent shave. She even smelt toothpaste on his breath. She thought his lips were like rosebuds and felt like holding each one between hers, just to feel the softness.

Earlier she had thought of Calum, what a strange encounter that was, their music already a powerful bond. Then Noel, no phone call. Noel was banished from her thoughts, into the doghouse.

She had plodded through her repertoire at the hotel to a smattering of applause and a proposition from the head waiter. The taxi outside tempted her and she was glad of its comfort. It would be nice to cook. To stay home and give the kitchen a rare work-out. She had about fifteen minutes before

Marcus arrived. Just enough time to transfer her gourmet packages from their polystyrene containers to china bowls.

They were in bed. She had been unfaithful to Noel. What had made her unfaithful to Noel? It was an animal, lusty, crazy longing. Now Marcus was holding her hair in his hand, pulling her down, eclipsing her face with his own. Her need for reassurance enhanced the sensations and she held onto him feeling again firmness, the magnetic force of his skin to hers.

Was it so bad after a year to love another man? It muddled her this jumbling of values, loyalties and sensations all in a huge melting pot that bubbled out a recipe of lust and release. Oh Noel, she thought, and felt she'd fouled her virgin self. Not a literal virgin, but all this time she had kept herself for him. What had made her change? What of the consequences, they would be more serious. How did it happen? Shouldn't she scramble out of his arms and tell Marcus it was all a mistake?

But his warmth, his scent, so different from Noel's, was not alien. She knew, if she wanted, he would stay, suggest they take the day off, go for a ride to the country, immerse themselves in the frivolities which new lovers indulged in. After all this time she had picked the night when Noel told her he was leaving.

Marcus looked young, almost angelic. What would they say to each other when he woke up? Was this justification for loneliness?

What Noel gave her was no longer enough. At first it was so easy, the wait fed her imagination, she could listen to her favourite music and think of how it would be, that moment when they next saw each other. He would summon her and she would go. It was always him, never the romance of the meeting place on which she built her scenario. If there wasn't Noel, would she, could she, love Marcus? He was asleep but each time she moved, his arm tightened around her. She knew if she got up he would wake. The pillow would absorb her, if she lay on it with the weight of her worries she would sink through it, through the bed into another world, the one she and Noel built for themselves and nobody else.

Should she tell Noel? Would she be the first to place a secret between them? If only she could distinguish between this abandon, weakness of flesh against flesh and the battering of indecision. She closed her eyes and imagined it was Noel, but Noel's hand was firmer, his skin not so soft, his belly podgy.

Marcus was awake, she caught the moment just before his eyes opened. His arm coiled around her and instead of enticing her into the trap she wanted to resist, he made no demands. He rolled over her and sprang up, looking at the time as if he was about to miss something important.

'Come on,' he said. 'Get dressed, we're going out.'

The intrigue, or was it weakness, a desire for risk or living dangerously threw her into his enthusiasm.

It had taken another hour to lose the main road and realize that the few small villages which clustered on the winding road were indicative of the type of place they were likely to find.

'Noel we better turn back, we'll never find anywhere here.'

It was completely dark and the road barely distinguishable from the curb. Every now and then they passed a few streetlights, which only accentuated how quiet and closed everything was around them. Their maps were not detailed enough to mark the villages they had already passed, and Noel had been hopelessly lost for the last three-quarters of an hour.

'I'll ask someone at the next café,' he said, which was another three villages down the road.

There was a place, about 15 kilometres further on, Noel phoned from the café and they had a room. The joy of luck sharpened his wits which were tired from the strain of driving endlessly into what he'd feared could become the void of the unknown. His only worry was losing his way, but only 15 kilometres, they would make it.

'Almighty Luck, Goddess of Luck, I thank you,' Noel said as, at last, he heaved himself out of the car, raised his arms to the sky and stopped short of kissing the ground when the door opened and a porter appeared.

It was a derelict-looking house in the middle of nowhere. The pointed roofs of its six small turrets caught the moonlight, hinting at generations of history. Mimosa drowned the entrance hall of cobblestone, guarded over by a portrait of the Madonna and Child. They could hear the clatter of knives and forks from the dining room and the heavy tread of waiters on the stone floor, as they were shown to the reception.

From the window of their room it was pitch black except for a shadow of a hanging branch. A whistle of wind blew and the silhouette of a shape floated away into the darkness. Rebecca closed the dusty red curtains whose weight had tugged at the rail and now slouched in a mass on the floor. A huge bed was decorated by what once must have been an exquisite hand-woven bedspread. Now it was still ornate but frayed and worn with threadbare patches, which had been covered by heaps of mismatched cushions. A small bright pink bathroom had escaped the time warp of the main room and shimmered from newly scrubbed porcelain and neat little packets of soap and a bathcap wrapped in plastic.

Noel lay on the bed which swallowed him into the softness of its mattress. He closed his eyes and felt them sting as he listened to the splatter of water as Rebecca's bath began to fill.

Later he followed the evening through again, from the time he had dozed off on the bed. It had seemed as if it must have been midnight by the time they had both bathed and changed and gone down to the dining room. But it couldn't have been that late because there were still guests waiting for the main course. There was a mysterious atmosphere about the place. It was one of the original monastery buildings, which had been sold to support rising costs, one of the waiters had said. In the morning they would see the old monastery and certainly hear the bell ringing for morning prayers. As they selected their cheeses and the dining room emptied Noel felt uneasy about the atmosphere. In the room, which was spartan but warm from an open fire, Noel had the strangest feeling that they were being watched.

Neither of them had said anything. They'd sipped and savoured a meal served with care and meticulous detail. Thick white tablecloths with solid cutlery and large white napkins. Wine from the region, tastes that enhanced the natural flavours of their choices. It was an adventure being there, in this unknown territory, the musky room whose walls must have listened to centuries of talk and seen the intimate lives of piety. He'd had a grappa, yes something the monks made, no he'd had two.

Then he was hazy. He tried to retrace his steps. He barely remembered leaving the dining room. What were they talking about? Rebecca had come to bed wearing a long white nightdress. He remembered how pale, almost white, her face had looked against her long black hair. She'd got into bed and his mind began to play. He felt a limb beside him and knew at once it was not hers.

Now as the light tried to steal through a gap in the curtains he saw the foolishness. Was it the drink that had distorted things? He had felt Briony as he got into bed. He had drunk in her scent, the room, the room had circled around him, the thick red curtains, the bed sinking, sinking and he'd held her to him, to save him. Briony was there, understanding, but his coarseness detroyed it all. Briony slithered into a faceless shadow, slipping through his fingers without giving him another chance. She was gone and in his arms was Rebecca, she was stroking his forehead and pulling the sheets up around his sweat, confining him with her calmness as if nothing had happened, as if everything was all right. He fought against it, against her understanding, and now it was daylight. She was wearing the white nightdress and her hair spun out around the pillow while she slept with the depth of a well-loved woman. The sun would not let him sleep. The sound of the birds, the shadowless day took over, while he asked himself as he watched and thought and felt, felt her so. Was it all a dream?

TWENTY-NINE

The days flashed by. First a week and then ten days. She had been on a fickle flight of fantasy: that was how she was going to explain it to Noel. Her longing for him had been overshadowed by the accessibility of Marcus who spoiled her thoroughly.

Briony was waiting for Noel to ring. The machine was manipulating things again. It didn't seem to work without her changing the message. Each changed message gave a detail of time. 'I'll be back this afternoon' the last message said. Noel had told her, please, to be there.

Noel was never far from her thoughts but Marcus had filled the gaps. She had expected the nights together would change their friendship for ever, but he made no demands nor seemed to expect anything. He had not even made her feel she should talk, tell him about Noel. He seemed more threatened by the machine. 'Leave it off,' he had said once, but she couldn't. Briony was not able to leave the flat without turning on the machine.

Noel was up to his old tricks. Hardly his fault, she didn't blame him, she was never there when he phoned.

One morning he had phoned and she cursed herself for not being there. It was the morning after she had been with Marcus. He must have known although he couldn't have at the time, when he had the nightmare. Noel had told her that he had stayed in a monastery that had been converted into a guest house. The atmosphere was eerie and cold. He had woken from a nightmare he couldn't escape. From then on his relationship with Rebecca had shattered. But it did not all fit together, his story. At first he begged the machine to get her to come to the phone and then he talked to it, and she noticed it calmed him down. He told the machine secrets, his own cross-thoughts, putting into words feelings that he'd never told her about, sharing confidences which made her jealous. The machine had them both in its control now. At first, when she denied it feelings, she knew she was the controller, but now with her weakness, this gnawing jealousy, its respect for her diminished. The machine not Noel told her to stay in. They were both waiting for him to phone.

The ring caught her heart on an off-beat and bored through her nervous system. She waited three rings.

'Oh! It's not the machine,' he said. 'I've written you a poem.'
'Who? Me?'
'No, the machine.' There was a long deep pause.
'Briony I have to see you, so much to talk about. I'm trying to get a flight a couple of days earlier. Meet me, will you? On our bridge. I know it must be awful for you, what strange presumption I have to expect you to wait for me, never to phone or ask questions. It will be different soon, I promise you.'
'Noel what's happened, have you changed your mind?'
'About you? No, I never did. I never knew I had made it up and I did long ago. Can you wait two more days? I'll make it up to you.
'Shall I read you the poem?

>
> 'I was a wave defying its ocean
> Breaking when the sea was calm
> Dancing alone in my foamy petticoat
> In secret, at night
> Always away,
> Away from the shore
> Until I saw you there
> On the forbidden stretch
> Bathing your toes in the circling pools
> Of someone else's wave

'And that's when I washed over you, rolled you up and took you out to sea away from everyone else.'

'You've been on the beach, haven't you?'

'Yes.'

'I am not going out with a wave!'

'You don't like my poem? All right then, what about changing it to a piece of driftwood, a lonely bit of driftwood who falls in love with a beautiful maiden with hair the colour of wholemeal spaghetti and eyes as dark as olives?'

'I can tell you are in Italy!'

'Noel . . .'

'What is it? Is everything all right? How's that Marcus? Is he looking after you? I don't know what you see in me. There's that good-looking bloke, rich, available and he adores you. I don't know what you see in me. But, my love, I can't wait to get home, no I am not going to tantalize myself.'

No matter how generous Rebecca was with the suntan lotion the first two days were always painful. She needed a small pink fry to form a base, otherwise she never got brown. Sunbathing by numbers seemed such a commerical infliction but she had to admit total block was the only cream which had ever stopped Noel burning.

She was glad of the sun and sea air to distract her from Noel's intolerable behaviour. Ever since that night in the monastery he had been unbearable. There had been something in that drink which had given him the qualities of a rabid dog. 'How did you get here?' he had asked her, when she was in the same bed. The next morning he looked sheepish as if he'd done something he shouldn't. And all the things he'd said in his sleep. He insisted they leave the next day immediately and wouldn't stop until they got back to the main road and were well en route for the coast.

There was an overwhelming sadness, which would flow through her in intermittent rushes, but she couldn't help thinking a few days without him would give her a chance to unknot herself. She still hadn't asked him the question.

Their days had settled into painful routine. Noel got up first and went for a walk along the beach. It was the only time he went near the beach, except sometimes he had lunch with her under the parasols. By the time he got back she would be up and they had breakfast together, either on the balcony or in the restaurant. There was nothing wrong with the hotel. Its white marble foyer was practical for sand-covered feet. Noel never liked large hotels and hated it at night when he heard voices from the room next door or the sounds of early morning plumbing.

After breakfast he took the car into the hills where he painted, sometimes for the whole day. Rebecca packed a beach bag and read or sewed, feeling the sand between her toes and every now and then swimming to the furthest raft. Once they went shopping, another time them went to the Hotel Splendido and basked in its quiet elegance, wishing they had been staying there but it was full and there was no way to change hotels.

At night they wandered to the restaurants in Portofino and talked about their days, although she never felt included when he talked. She'd left it too late to ask him now, she would have to wait until he said something.

Last night he told her he'd had enough, that he wanted to go home and that was where he was now, at the travel agent changing his ticket. She didn't mind, there was nothing to salvage here. She had been wrong about the sun and the rest, it was far more serious.

Noel had wanted to change his ticket before he phoned Briony. He wanted to see her to get her seal of approval and then he would tell Rebecca. He should have said something already. He knew how he had hurt Rebecca but she seemed strangely at peace, not agitated and nervous. He hated this deceit, but he was to blame, he was the deceiver, it was cowardly to push her to the edge so she'd do his dirty work for him. His thoughts turned to dreams of nocturnal meanderings. Only once had they, Briony and he, had a morning together and now there would be two, maybe three. How could he account for his disappearance while Tammy was at home? Perhaps he'd get away with it, if he didn't tell anyone, they'd still think he was away unless Rebecca phoned home.

He paid the extra money and watched the girl input the relevant information into the computer. He hated those words, input, relevant documents, chips. He centred on her bright red nail varnish, noticing how she had developed a way of typing, clipping her nails over the keys so she didn't chip the polish. His ticket popped up and he followed it as she checked the information and placed it crisply inside a folder into which she added a few labels and a print-out of his itinerary. 'Thank you, Mr Kenilmore, have a pleasant trip.' She smiled with vacant blue eyes beyond whose misty film he detected more life. A new life: that was what he held. He went to take the ticket out, to look at it, and saw a telephone booth across the street. In his haste, sandwiched by a dream, he looked the wrong way before he crossed, realizing his mistake a little too late.

Briony was to say afterwards 'What car did you hit?' Then she asked what colour it was. Even he could not see how he could be consoled by the fact that the car, no matter that it was one of his least favourite colours, was off the road. She did, he had to admit, succeed in getting his mind off the pain.

He was mowed down by a Fiat taking its owners to the beach. Noel walked into the road looking in the other direction giving the car a slim chance to swerve. It started too late and as it did so it nicked his bottom, throwing him into the road. Still holding his ticket he foolishly put out his right hand to break his fall: exactly what he had learned not to do when he once trained for a parachute jump. Fortunately there was no back-up to further splatter his already crumpled form. He heard the brakes as the car stopped and a patter of sandals on the tarmac and then rapid conversation. When they found he was English the voices hushed in caution but by this time Noel was feeling the pain. The ambulance came, it looked more like a hearse and Noel was strapped into a stretcher. Where was the hospital: it was not the sort of place you tried to find when on holiday. He remembered wondering which of the girls he should phone first, but then the shot he'd been given, in his arm, he would always say in his recounting of the story, obliterated his consciousness and his sense of humour.

THIRTY

The recital was in four days. She would be adamant and insist on practising tonight. Each time he had wheedled her round. This time Marcus could have tickets to Rio and she would not go.

Briony was waiting to hear from Noel. She was going to surprise him by meeting him at the airport. She could imagine him coming through customs, not knowing where he put his passport, flattened by guilt as he would be sure to think he had something to declare.

The phone rang.

'Marcus, hello.'

'Briony, look I'm sorry I have to go away for two days, there's been a problem.'

'What is it, Marcus?'

'Nothing, one of the charities has gone bankrupt they need me to sort it out. I'm sorry, I'll miss you. Keep on practising: it's only a few days to go.'

'I know, Marcus. I'll see you when you get back.'

It served her right, she thought, jumping to conclusions. No explanations would be necessary. He was leaving as Noel arrived. She still didn't believe Noel would do it. In all the time she had known him there was always a reason why he could not get away, a lie covering a lie. Somehow with an alibi, it became a distortion of the truth, more plausible. She loved the idea of him being in the audience. If he did catch his plane he'd see some of her life, meet a few friends. Marcus was the only person he had ever met. Their lives were so separate she wondered what they would be like together, merged, moulded into each other. She closed her eyes and allowed herself to think of Noel. She thought of some of his expressions, the funny clothes he wore, neither modern nor conservative, the way he talked about his work, the things he told her when they went to an exhibition together, his doubts, his ideas, his ability to turn something mundane into a pumpkin studded with gold or an open-ended tunnel, mysterious and magic.

She was highly strung and ran for much of the time on nervous energy. At the moment she could eat anything and be hungry again in no time. Now with Noel showing up, she just had to think of seeing him and feel light-headed. There was the recital as well, she worried about keeping her feet on the ground. She'd worked hard and was confident of her programme, she knew seeing Noel would give her that edge to sharpen the Rachmaninov. She went to practise and turned up the phone in case he rang and she didn't hear. She was surprised he hadn't phoned by now, especially since the flight he was trying to get left that evening.

Rebecca was oblivious to time, although she was beginning to recognize the patterns of the sun. Now that she knew its heat she judged the day by it, watching it in the sky, knowing long before it cast the first evening shadows what time of day it was.

She had been fairly sure of Noel having lunch with her. He said he was leaving in the evening or first thing the next day. She was not going to let it worry her. If he hadn't showed by two o'clock she would have lunch and then walk to Portofino.

The waiter had served her melon and her spoon was slipping through the soft pulp. She remembered the moment exactly because she had not been sure what to order and settled on the melon. When searching her memory she was aware of one of the hotel staff coming towards the restaurant and talking to her waiter. She saw their nervous glances directed at her, then they came up to her table and she realized something was wrong.

They had no details of Noel, only that he had been in an accident and taken to hospital. The hotel phoned the hospital while she changed. There was no information except that the doctor was with Noel. Her fears multiplied during the taxi ride.

Noel had been given a generous dose of whatever it was that knocked him out, so he was barely aware of reaching the hospital, being wheeled out of the ambulance and slapped on a stretcher. As the effect of the drug diminished he suffered an onslaught of pain and found himself surrounded by a number of masked Italian doctors. 'Don't cut anything off without my consent,' he had told the doctor. Then he must have been given something else to ease the pain because when he next woke up he was in a ward, not feeling at all bad.

It was a dramatic turn of events and the most expensive broken arm in the Western hemisphere, Noel said when he recounted the accident. Not even a bad break but a clean uncomplicated snap in his lower right arm, which was a blessing as he was left-handed.

The news had not sounded as good to Rebecca, who arrived while he was on an operating table. Fortunately everyone spoke English, they even had cappuccino. The doctor came out as Noel was being wheeled upstairs. 'Ee as ad a nasty boomp,' the doctor said, his grammatically correct English disguised by a native tongue. Noel had broken his arm, he confirmed, and there was a chance of concussion, but it was slim. He was to stay overnight and if all went well he could go home tomorrow. Rebecca stayed by his bedside until Noel woke up. It seemed as if she was there for hours.

In his hazy state Noel felt relieved to see Rebecca, a familiar face. The hospital was more comfortable than an NHS equivalent and he hadn't had to sign anything yet. God, what was it all going to cost? He let his hand rest in Rebecca's and then thought, 'Oh, My God. Briony.'

There were insurance details to sort out. Rebecca had the

policies with her and ploughed through the fine print, hoping they would not have to pay up front and get reimbursed later. No fat chance. Not only that, in the office of admissions she found the only person in the hospital who didn't speak English.

It was tiring, the accident, the hospital, the trauma, the paperwork. Thank God Noel was all right. It did seem it was just a break. He urged her to go back to the hotel, get some sleep and pick him up the next day.

After Rebecca left, Noel's mind buzzed. He must get a message to Briony. What if she'd gone to the airport? No she wouldn't have done that because he hadn't decided on a flight when he last talked to her. But she might have phoned the airline, checked the passenger list. He knew she'd know something was wrong.

He was not to move, the doctor said. But Noel insisted on making the phone call. They got him into a wheelchair and set him up with the phone. As he dialled he felt his dream fade away, dissolve, absorbed into the air like the short life of a soap bubble. There was no chance of him going to Briony now.

They were strong, her fingers. The muscles had built up from constant practising but now they ached. Briony looked at the time, she had been playing for almost five hours. She shook her hands out and hung them loose by her side. Occasionally she had stopped to damn Noel for keeping her in suspense. Why hadn't he phoned? Now there was no chance of him arriving tonight. What had happened?

She blamed herself, condemned herself for messing about with Marcus. By now she was convinced something serious was wrong. It was simple. By not asking for anything, Marcus was demanding more. He knew he could provide what Noel could not: time together. Or was Marcus what Noel was not: younger, free, and did she like it? No wonder she was practising so well today. Who would want such ambiguity playing in their mind?

She stretched, making herself as tall as she could, and then the phone rang.

The first ring finished, then the second and the third. She was paralysed, come on, come on, she said to herself, four rings, and then she picked it up. His voice had a false sense of jolliness and then he told her about the accident.

'Which arm?' That was all she could say. The image of Noel ruffled and creased over an Italian road while she was miles away, oblivious and helpless, no help to him at all. He could have died and she would not know. She'd never thought that before. If he died the only way she would have of knowing would be if she read it in the papers. That hit a chord and it reverberated like a peal of church bells, irritating church bells that rang when you didn't want to hear them.

'My dearest one, I'm sorry, it is such a loss to me, not seeing you. I don't know when I'll see you. I'll have to come back with Rebecca on Saturday. What about Sunday, as soon as I get home?'

'Noel, I can't. That's the recital. Monday, I'll wait until then, you get better, my love.'

'I'm sorry too. So sorry that I can't be there, that I can never be there.'

'Can you still draw?'

'I don't know; I expect so. I'm in a wheelchair at the moment. Lovely nurses these Italian girls, with their curls and long black hair, olive skin . . . !'

'Doesn't look as if you will be there long enough to get to know them.'

'I'll have to wait until Monday, on the bridge, that's where we will meet. I might not be able to phone you again.'

They consoled themselves with light talk to cheer each other up.

'How's Adolph?' he said.

'She, Adolphe, has been angelic, we miss you.'

'Yes, I know. I have missed you too much not to change

things.' Now she couldn't hang up. Don't go, she thought as they hung on saying nothing. She saw him, in a hospital bed. She wanted to tell him everything, she didn't want his understanding just forgiveness, this overbearing feeling of wanting everything to be right again.

For a long time after they hung up she sat quite silent on the piano stool. Marcus had taken her mind off the only thing she cared about, the only person she wanted to think about.

Rebecca couldn't help herself. She saw the funny side of it and burst out laughing in the cocktail lounge. Well, it was. There was Noel planning to leave her on the Riviera while he leapt back for some secret rendezvous and he ends up flat on his back with a broken arm. She laughed again, which she saw caught the eyes of the waiters.

At first when she got back to the hotel all she wanted to do was go to bed but she mustered up the energy to bath and change, and now she was drinking a whisky sour.

'You are alone?'

The voice came from a well-packed man probably approaching his fifties. He wore an exquisitely cut and tailored suit.

'No, not exactly, my husband is in hospital.'

'Oh how terrible. Please, I didn't mean to disturb you.'

'It's quite all right. Nothing serious, just a bit of a shock. He was knocked down by a car and broke his arm.' She laughed again. She couldn't help it, what a wicked thing to do.

'I'm sorry,' she said. 'It's just that, well, I don't know, I suppose it was the shock and the strain and then, I'm probably over-tired.'

'Perhaps you need something to eat?'

'Yes probably, I was going into the dining room when I'd finished my drink.'

'May I escort you? I am on my own tonight as well.'

His name was Vittorio and he came from Milan, although he considered himself French. He had been to university in Paris, worked and lived there, and considered it home. 'Many Italians do not like the French, but I love them,' he told her. He had been in Paris at the same time Rebecca was there, he stoked old memories fondly.

Briefly they touched upon Noel but he was in and out of their conversation quickly. Starved for company, Rebecca was enchanted, just the chance to talk to someone and the friendship which comes from a stranger is always uncomplicated, unbiased, exciting.

The meal ended too quickly. Vittorio escorted her to her room. He shook hands. 'Perhaps I will see you at breakfast tomorrow?'

'I doubt it. I have to get up early, to pick my husband up from hospital.' They left it at that.

Noel slept badly knowing a good night's sleep would speed his recovery and get him out of this ghastly place. The smell: he couldn't bear how hospitals everywhere smell the same, of antiseptic and powerful cleaning agents trying to fend off disease. This night spent in his narrow bed against a background of clattering dentures, wizened bedmates and Italian snores enhanced his fear of impending mortality. All right, he was exaggerating, but he was certainly not the youngest in this ward. Perhaps they were keeping him here because something major was wrong and they were running tests to be sure before they told him. He pulled at his skin and let it fall to see how wrinkly he was. For a man his age it was still firm, quite firm. His teeth were good, slightly receding gums but nothing to worry about his dentist said. His hair was highlighted with grey but he was used to that. Or was he?

Anyone would feel the same in a foreign hospital, he told himself. The food was good and the coffee. And pretty nurses, except they all spoke Italian. But he hadn't had a single injection in his bum. No one would believe him of course, everyone thought the continentals aways leapt at the chance to stick a needle in your arse.

He heard the squeak of wheels on the linoleum as a nurse approached with the pill trolley. He heaved his plastered arm. How long was he going to have this on? How was he going to hug Briony when he saw her? What an idiot not looking. It could have been much worse; small consolation. The nurse was coming. He'd nail her for some drugs, something to get him to sleep. He could do with a brandy but it was about four in the morning. He waved with his good arm and gesticulated his requirements. She spoke perfectly good English. A light flirtation livened his spirits. Perhaps he should stay here. There's an idea. Send Rebecca back to England and he'd stay here.

Another day, two more mornings and then home. What was she going to do with Noel? He could sit on the balcony and sketch. Rebecca phoned the hospital who were ready to release him. She poked her head in the breakfast room before she left but there was no sign of Vittorio.

When she arrived Noel was dressed and sitting in a wheelchair. He needed to rest for a day or two but then he would be fine for the flight home. 'It is not my feerst cast that has gone to England,' the doctor said.

Noel was quite happy to be propped up in bed and waited on. He stayed in the room all day urging Rebecca to go the beach, not to waste the last days of sun.

By the evening he still did not want to get up. Rebecca decided to go downstairs for dinner alone. She waited for room service to bring Noel's supper and then went to the cocktail lounge. It was too sweet, the whisky sour, but she drank it anyway. She finished her drink and looked at her watch. How foolish, she thought, what am I doing? She thanked the barman and went to the restaurant.

Vittorio approached her with the same smoothness, the same perfect manners as last night, shortly after the waiter had taken her order.

'You are alone again, may I join you? Please do not be polite if you wish to be alone.'

She was glad to have someone to recount the day's events to. They picked up from yesterday, he telling her about his life and she telling him about hers. It was unusual that, normally she talked about their life, hers and Noel's, but now it was hers.

He was looking to buy a villa for the holidays. Today he had seen something he liked and he asked her if tomorrow she might like to see it. She agreed and they arranged to meet.

It was the last full day of their holiday. Rebecca looked tanned and healthy, a spark was again in her eyes and her hair, black and shiny, had caught the sun, which brought out a few red highlights. Noel had changed colour from white to peach, he was losing weight, which was expedited by the broken arm saga. He decided to go down to the beach and thought the two of them might have lunch together. Rebecca was going to tell him about Vittorio and then decided not to. 'I'm going shopping,' she said. 'But I'll help you get settled first.'

Noel was up but wobbly. He had a bruise the size of a watermelon on his right side from the car and a few less dramatic reminders. Stiffness was setting in and it hurt him to move. He staggered onto his crutches and the two of them made a slow procession across the hotel and to the beach. Now that he was dependent on her, Noel was more manageable. She probably should not be going anywhere with a man she hardly knew, thought Rebecca, but she was not about to change her mind.

The villa was half an hour away, up into the hills which looked onto a small bay. There was a swimming pool, barbecue patio and small, densely foliated terrace, which the renovated farmhouse overlooked. It was idyllic but not whimsical. Vittorio was separated until an appropriate settlement decided the divorce. He had been married before but a long time ago. His two children from his second entanglement needed a place like this, he said, for the holidays. Since they lived in Paris he wanted to get somewhere in Italy so they would be fluent in Italian.

Bougainvillea trailed in an unruly way across a natural brick wall and the hibiscus was in flower, red and blood orange. Although no one was living there now, a gardener watered it every day and the fruits of his labour were in full cry.

'It's lovely, much more than that, it has a certain character, it feels good and friendly.'

'Yes, it is a special place, I thought you would like it. Let's go now and have some lunch.'

When it was five o'clock and the waiters sat down at a far table to eat before the evening meal Rebecca thought of Noel. She must get back. Vittorio knew that, she could tell. Almost immediately he asked for the bill and then they were back in the car on the way back. He dropped her at the hotel and went to the car park.

'Thank you, for a marvellous afternoon. I will not see you tonight, I'm having dinner with friends. Goodbye Rebecca.'

He was gone and the next day she was leaving. She didn't even know his surname. Why should it worry her this chance meeting? Something which could never be more than a brief encounter.

There was not much of Noel that didn't hurt. Foolishly he had fallen asleep in the sun, without his total block, whilst wearing his sunglasses. At least he had kept his shirt on so his chest avoided sizzling but it was now quite a different colour from his extremities. When Rebecca showed no sign of returning he had eaten his lunch at the beach restaurant. They managed to bring a telephone to his table and he had spent most of the time talking to the answering machine. They were such friends by now that they had much in common. He had chatted to it first in Italian and then lapsed into his native tongue. The answering machine was quite a linguist. He described each bruise leaving the watermelon until last adding 'I'm not telling you this for sympathy, you know? Well I better go, it must be time for another pain killer.'

THIRTY-ONE

The news of Noel's accident threw her up against an imaginary wall where the bang had a splintering effect. What dangerous games they had both been playing with lives, wrapping the truth in an airtight bag.

All those nights with Marcus in the weird and exotic places, the low-life which he seemed to have some connection with. The extremes, his wealth and fascination with poverty. That was him, but she had been with him, mesmerized by the same things he showed her, equally able to adapt. To dance and drink champagne wearing high heels and décolleté dresses one night and footless tights and greaseball hair the next. Carried away without thinking, away from routine, mundacity, that was not a word, but it was what she meant, the mundane things that everybody does because they have to. She had pretended all this time that Noel was not important. She had acted as if he was, but to herself, she always convinced herself that he wasn't and in the end who had she fooled? Nobody except herself.

She was glad to be alone, to realize she must tell Noel what they were to each other. No matter if it changed the perfect conception of their love. Perhaps they didn't call it that, but there wasn't another word which came as close. That was part of it, denying that love existed, it was all part of the same charade. They had come to a point in a full circle where they would have to decide. She remembered joking, asking him if he would die for her. It was really a joke. Nobody died like that any more, not unless it was tax efficient. No, now there was a worse form of dying, to die while you were still living. She could wait until Monday. She couldn't wait any longer to tell him they must take the risk.

They were leaving, and suddenly it seemed like an eternity since Rebecca struggled across the gravel in her high-heeled shoes. Again it was sunny and she knew exactly what the day would have in store for her if she were to stay, except if she had seen Vittorio.

To think she was so convinced that he would kiss her. But he did nothing. Shook her hand twice and in the car touched her shoulder lightly as he left her at the hotel. He had disappeared. Last night when Noel and she had dinner she thought she might see him, in the bar, but he never came.

Noel had gone downstairs to settle the bill and she looked at the packed suitcases as if it was her life with Noel about to be locked up. A wave of nostalgia rattled by and she thought all she was taking home was a tan. The porter came and took the bags. She walked onto the balcony and watched the tideless waves unravel themselves like hair released from its curler. Boats zigzagged by in silence, the distance cutting out the sound of their motors. One of the hotel staff helped a couple into a pedalo, the water-ski man flashed his muscle. She turned back into the room, picked up her new mink-coloured handbag and without turning back walked out.

When the bill came Noel wanted to pay it quickly, it was the telephone calls he was worried about. He wanted to settle before Rebecca came down and he wanted to send Briony a telegram, to wish her luck on Sunday. How thoughtless, he hadn't even asked her where she was playing. It was huge, of course, the telephone bill, itemised day by day. At least it didn't have the number printed on it. The cashier was taking ages, and there was Rebecca. It was luck, Noel thought, someone was talking to Rebecca. She turned to look in his direction.

'I won't be a moment, love. Why don't you go and order us both a coffee?' Noel said.

They went to the garden, glad of last minutes together.
'That's your husband,' said Vittorio.
'Yes, you noticed the plaster.'
'Rebecca, I am sorry but I wanted to see you again, to say goodbye, to give you my card, my name, in case you might ever want to see me again.'
'Thank you, yes, I was hoping to see you before I left.'
'I hope we will meet again, I hope very much,' he said and then he kissed her hand and was gone leaving his warmth on her hand where he had held it.

'That's all sorted out,' said Noel. 'Who was that man?'
'Oh just someone who talked to me, the night you were in hospital.'
'We better go,' said Noel. 'It's quite a long drive to the airport.'

THIRTY-TWO

Briony had quelled her disappointment through concentration. For once she avoided distractions. The only person she had seen in the last two days was Calum.

Noel would be home today. She went through the programme, still not satisfied. Later she was having her last lesson with Natalie who wanted her to play straight through, mistakes, hiccups, slurs. Marcus was picking her up at 11 o'clock the next day. She was confident about the Rachmaninov piece, now it was Grieg who made her feel anxious. She decided to listen to recordings and then play herself. This would be the last time she listened for fear of being influenced. Calum certainly did play the clarinet well.

Tonight Lizzie was coming to Marengo's, she found herself even more detached than the last time they met. She wanted an early night and could see how that idea was not going to work out. They were rampant, her thoughts, not sequential, if only she could concentrate on the present.

The music, the music, the music. What would she wear tomorrow? Marcus said it was black tie. Black tie for a lunch, who were these people? Obviously rich, old fashioned and traditional; she imagined the house would be dripping in period furniture. They had a Steinway that unnerved her. It was difficult adapting to another piano. Natalie suggested a long dress but she decided that was a little too formal. She agreed on looking professional, treating it as if it were something far more official. What foresight to get her hair done, that would give her some relaxation before her performance. She would have it plaited with hair pulled from the side of her face, and woven together like embroidery, but not fancy. The pale blue dress, that was perfect with the matching short-waisted jacket. She went to dig it out, it was so long since she'd worn it. Sleeveless with delicate beadwork around the neckline it was formal enough and the satin shoes she'd dyed to go with it were fine for the pedals. She had even played a Steinway before wearing those shoes.

There would be fewer people at the party than at Marengo's but this was more important. She and the piano alone. In one way she longed for the challenge but there was no question: if she did not play well these people would let her know. Less than a day. She hoped she wouldn't have to talk to anyone at the party, she must tell Marcus that, he could do all the talking. She was far too nervous already. Noel would definitely be home by now, if only he would ring.

'Oh machine, can't you get him to phone?' It was funny the machine. She'd grown quite fond of it while Noel was away. She could see how Noel came to depend on it. She had given up using it except for him. All her friends had complained that it was always busy, her phone, but usually it was Noel talking to the machine. She could never retrieve her messages when she went out because most days Noel left messages that were twenty minutes or so long and she never had enough change to listen to it all. Sometimes it infuriated her. 'All right, I won't phone any more,' he said, but he couldn't keep away from it.

'I am now going to practise,' she told the machine, as if its watchful eye would make her keep her word.

Noel was opening the post. There was a pile for bills, one for possible work, another for letters people wrote about his work, and miscellaneous. He predicted them before he opened them to ease the tedium of coming home to so many bills. 'Miscellaneous' he said to himself as he opened a much squarer envelope than the standard size. He read it once and then twice, feeling himself brim with pride. Who could he tell, but yet keep it quiet? It was a milestone, he had been asked to exhibit two paintings in the Tate Gallery, he'd been asked to sit at the high table of art.

He phoned Briony; she wasn't there; he told the machine anyway. Rebecca, he found her in the kitchen and told her the good news. 'That's wonderful,' she said, meaning every word, but it was a surface enthusiasm which didn't come close to the whooping in Noel's stomach. 'You haven't forgotten Sophia's party this afternoon, have you?' He'd forgotten all about it.

Rebecca hadn't though, she'd nurtured her tan for it. Normally quite modest about her appearance Rebecca wanted to look stunning. She had bought the ochre suit with the party in mind; she was even having her hair done. Ever since her meeting with Vittorio she felt it important to make an effort, keep up appearances and standards. Her independence was lapping at her feet, she couldn't ignore it. She had decided to take the job, to branch out. If she had learned anything on holiday it was that her life had changed. Now instead of watching, waiting for what inevitably lay in store, she was choosing her own direction. She wondered whether to have her hair up, coiled in a chignon, but then thought that too tight. No, she'd have it loose and curled, cascading down her back.

It was raining, for the garden party. The blue satin shoes would be ruined on a wet English lawn. The pale pinks and lemons, flimsy dresses and open-toed shoes would fade in the damp, soggy, cloud-filled garden. They would have to light fires inside and create the first warmth against winter instead of the last moments of summer.

Briony pulled her dressing gown around her just as the intercom buzzed.

It was the postman with a package. 'Thank you.'

There was a telegram which she tore open. It was from Noel.

'Play well, my dearest love, play from your heart. Until the bridge where I shall be waiting. Only hours apart, my love, from yours.'

The package, was a book he'd sent from Florence. 'I couldn't get the chime but this is where it would have come from!' he'd written on a note.

Right up again her spirits lifted, even the sky was lighter. She didn't have time to dwell on such things. Hairdresser in half an hour, time to change and then Marcus would be there. Maybe the sky would clear. She should eat something: no, there would be mountains of food at the party.

She worked it out, what she would wear if the weather was damned, while sitting under the hair dryer. By thinking hard, by willing the air to somehow rearrange itself, to make the day all right, it had worked. When she left the sky was blue.

Sometimes when she put make-up on it was bad and sometimes good. There was no logic. At first she thought it was if she rushed, or if she was tired, but it was something more than that. She knew when she woke up whether her eyes would glint or have a dull glazed look. That was one of the reasons she wanted to take up jogging, but she simply didn't have the will power, well no, she didn't like it enough, that was all.

Her make-up brushes reminded her of Noel, but this was a delicate operation, a little bit of colour and mascara. She needed to look good for the extra confidence it would give her. She was already wearing the dress. She knew it was backwards to get dressed first, in case she spilt something but she liked the finishing touch to be a dab of lipstick and then see the whole effect. It wasn't the same if she was standing in a camisole and stockings. That was something she always wanted: a silk camisole and french knickers, but it wasn't something you buy for yourself nor something you hint at for a present, so she had never had one.

The buzzer made her jump and she felt hurried and unprepared. Just nerves, because in another five minutes she'd be pacing the room.

Marcus looked debonaire? She couldn't think of the right word to describe his looks although she was sure it began with 'D' delicious, desirable, dapper.

'You look fabulous, fantastic,' he said. 'All "F" words,' she thought. 'Hello Briony, I've missed you.' And he kissed her gently, aware of her fragile nerves.

'Ready? Let's go and we'll stop for coffee somewhere on the way.'

Each pebble of gravel looked as if it had been individually polished. They hissed and spun under the wheels of the car, lining up in their thousands, bordering the hill which led to the house.

The setting oozed opulence. Rays of sun bounced off the polished chrome of a collection of classic cars which congregated like nesting sparrows around the far corner of the drive, and the house, unimpressed, watching over it all.

It was a beautiful house, its old grey stone dipped in time and carefully selected greenery, a little ivy, moss creeping into crevices, staring over the unspoilt green of rolling hills dotted with sheep and clusters of trees.

'Come on,' said Marcus. 'Are you ready?'

He opened the door and Briony heard the rustle of skirts and hurried footsteps.

'Hello Master Marcus, it's good to see you again.'

'Hello Adele, this is Briony.'

She was on her guard suddenly, this familiarity unnerving, she racked her brains to remember details, he had said good friends – 'these longtime friends?' – she couldn't remember.

They walked down a wood-panelled corridor coated with dark shady portraits into a large drawing room with a side of french doors leading outside. The view poured out beyond her and she feasted her eyes on every detail. The grass mowed with the fine weave of a Persian carpet, its smell competing with banks of roses coquettishly tossing their scent up to the sun. Down by the river, boats draped in twisted ribbons swung on the water. Nearby white parasols shaded tables glistening in white linen and myriads of tiny violets. The trees bowed in the slight breeze, lending their branches to the whims of the wind.

Marcus watched her, soaking it in, her eyes dilated, her hand unconsciously squeezing his, she did not speak. He led her towards a group of people. A yellow dress she saw floating, hats, trimmed with ribbons, flowers and the men so elegant in white dinner jackets, one had a black rose in his lapel, another dark kind eyes, she liked the eyes on this older man. They lit as Marcus approached and she saw a smile creep across his face, then the eyes burst like a kaleidoscope into animation. 'Marcus'. He took hold of Marcus' hand with both of his and clutched him vehemently. Then, so as not to leave her standing there solitary, he offered his strong warm hand. 'So this is the lady: Briony, isn't it? She is as pretty as you said.'

'Briony,' said Marcus, 'this is my father, Darwin Eccleston.'

They were late, over an hour late and Rebecca cursed Noel silently as she memorized the embossed invitation on her lap in an attempt to control herself: 'Lord and Lady Eccleston request the pleasure of your company.' The idea of anyone requesting Noel's company at the moment was a hideous thought. She was so angry she could feel the anger pummelling against her rib cage, rearing to get out, attack, launch itself at its originator.

Noel looked uncomfortable and out of place. He looked like a cardboard cut-out, starched and immobile in his dinner jacket. That was why they were late. He had refused, point blank refused, to wear it and she would not accept such childish behaviour. Now that it was on, even he liked the way he looked, but not the principle. This was why she was angry, she was sure the principle would reiterate throughout the day. She was certain Noel had not thought how formal and Establishment this would be and against the grain it would gnaw. She would leave him as soon as she had the chance, he could paddle his own canoe.

Briony was out of her depth. She had met Marcus' step-mother, Sophia, and realized the significance of his bringing her here to meet his parents. She knew what she had suspected and tried to ignore was true. Marcus wanted to marry her. The undercurrent she was swimming against now was why she had been asked to play the piano. Had Marcus thought of her playing as a ploy to get her here? The idea of her playing would be a farce if that was true. At least now she knew where he got his money from. So this house would one day be his.

Marcus was trying to prise her away, it was he who was in suspense. Briony liked Sophia although she seemed an unlikely companion for Darwin, who she liked but imagined must be a tyrant to live with. Certainly used to getting his own way. The jigsaw pieces were falling into place, but she could see Marcus was impatient and edging towards her, she didn't have much longer.

'Sophia, let me steal Briony for a moment, I want to show her the river.' He marched her to the dock, chose a rowing boat and pushed off.

'I know what you are thinking.'

'No, you don't,' she said.

'It's the recital, isn't it?'

'Perhaps you won't believe it, but that was how it began. My father asked me if I knew anyone talented enough to play today, no run of the mill, out-of-work musician,' he said. 'Someone special, I don't mind how much it costs. I thought of you. He asked me first and I fell in love with you later, after I had asked you to play.'

'Marcus, I . . .'

'Briony, please give me a chance. I know you and Noel, you

two belong to each other, you will have to decide what you are going to do but I had to tell you what I feel.'

In that moment she almost loved him, forgave him, pitied him, thinking herself ignorant and stupid.

'I don't know, Marcus. I think, nothing, everything! I am lucky to have you in my life. It's a shock, meeting your father here like this. You didn't tell me anything. It's so peaceful one of the most beautiful places I have ever been to.'

'You're not angry?'

'No, how could I be?' He put down the oars to thank her, while the water lapped softly around the boat.

'We better head back. They'll all be looking for the piano player.'

The lawn was covered in checks of colour when they returned. Briony caught a glimpse of Sophia's white ruched dress sprinkled with pink bows, and the moments on the river, their intimacy, was lost. The squares moved around them strategically as on a board game. Everyone knew Marcus, family friends wanted to catch up on news, mutual friends in common. She was passed from one to another, 'This is Briony, Briony meet Sir Roland Jollop, Emma Simms, Jocelyn Bucannan.' Again and again she shook hands as the dresses, suits, jackets shuffled around them.

Then she saw him coming towards them, intangible as a phantom in a dream, they would be sure to meet if only she could reach to stop him. She felt stifled as if her dress was inwardly devouring her, closing off the air. She wanted to run into his arms but her feet remained firmly planted. Marcus saw and in that frozen moment felt her hand in his break into a sweat, he felt the heat rise as he watched them fail to disguise their attraction. The silks of the crowd dissolved and they were left standing, the four of them, out of place, filled with apprehension.

Marcus slapped Noel on the back finding a suitable flow of clichés covering him. 'You've met Briony?' and they were forced to shake hands, which they did like waxworks to hide the effect of their touch. 'We haven't met,' Marcus said to Rebecca. 'I'm Marcus Eccleston.'

'I'm sorry,' said Noel, clutching at the situation. 'This is my wife Rebecca.' Then he introduced Briony, 'I'm afraid I've forgotten your surname.'

'Briony Lange,' she said as she shook hands with Rebecca. Their silence was caught within a few pleasantries.

'Briony, people are going into the drawing room, it's probably time for you to play.'

'Yes, of course.' Rebecca asked what she was playing and she told her, trying to avoid Noel's eyes.

'That's the girl on the answering machine,' said Rebecca. 'I recognize her voice.'

The people were crowding in, far more than she expected, and Briony felt as if they were coming to a hanging, her hanging, and Noel the executioner would string her up from the gallows. She knew at once that Marcus had not expected to see Noel. Why had she not said where she was playing? She shook out her fingers in anticipation. The music had to be her salvation. She longed to reach the piano, it would save her. She was in a blur; the music was hanging around in her head; she would have to put it back, mix it up with what had just gone in, channel it through her mind, let her soul grab hold of it. As if she had punched in a code and opened a safe door she worked on automatic, gliding to the piano as if in a trance. Taking her time she sat down, adjusted the stool the way she did at home and announced the pieces she was playing. She heard the silence spin a web catching the occasional cough, before she filled it with her playing, bursting and melting phrases within the room.

Noel was at the back, alone, the confrontation no doubt due later. It was the best she had ever played and her music reached over to calm him, lassoing and drawing him closer. Through the open door he saw a telephone on a sideboard in the hall. It was far enough away for him to ring without disturbing anyone but he still whispered into the mouthpiece. 'Listen Briony, listen to yourself play.'

Briony knew he had heard the Rachmaninov, she knew it, she'd got to the heart of the piece and it gave her pleasure to ride on euphoria when she finished. She played two pieces after that, one a request, and stopped on the crest of applause. She looked around, but Noel had gone.

THIRTY-THREE

The crispness of approaching autumn cut the air around a vast sea of solid cobalt. Every spire loomed sharp against this backdrop, below a sun-baked polish gave the Thames an asphalt sheen. Noel was standing, lolling with his arms resting on the bridge, each soaring seagull, passing boat, rhythmic tap of heels on the tarmac, attracting his attention. Now that he had made a decision he could rest from the constant weighing up, the toing and froing. How had Rebecca known about the answering machine? Why hadn't she said more? Now he knew that she knew, but neither of them had said anything. He folded his arms, the good one resting on his cast looking out towards St Paul's. He wanted Briony to come up to him, to feel her before their eyes had to meet because he knew they would be filled with the complications they had to unravel.

Briony was confused, that now, after all this time, he'd changed his mind. When they met it would be quite different because it was loaded, loaded with everything their affair had dismissed, money, children, mortgage payments. Leave me alone. She thought about this lethal dose of reality. Put Noel back on his white charger. Leave him with his doubts and uncertainties with his silly self in a pair of boxers and those tasteless fluorescent socks, and then she saw him standing there.

One step forward two steps back, she would never get closer. In the distance she could see him, holding onto the railing with both hands. At last he turned and she saw him start to run. That was the answer, to run, and as she did, she broke out of the mould, she began to get closer.

So many days had passed since they last met. It was years since she had seen him but he looked the way she imagined, no disappointment, no hyperbole. Everything she'd saved up to tell him, trivia mostly, about things they had in common, misadventures that he would associate with, they all went out of her mind. They reached each other and stuck, nuzzling under layers of clothing leaning on one another's stability, both wishing they hadn't wasted so much time pulling apart what had been inevitable.

'We will put a table between us and you will tell me everything, everything you've thought, everything you have done and then I will tell you why and how I am leaving my wife.' He bent down and from his bag took two beakers and a small bottle of champagne.

'Let's drink to us, if you will have me.'

When she told him about Marcus his eyes dropped. They sunk low and small folds of skin gathered up under them as if preparing to catch a tear.

'I don't love him, Noel. I thought if I couldn't have you everything else would be a compromise. Where do you start and where do you stop when you decide to compromise?'

He had almost been too late. She couldn't wait for ever, holding her life back for him, although she would never have said so. He imagined how it would happen, the change gradual, the gap would widen between their lives together and time apart. Her life was teetering on change, he could tell. He had seen the faces and heard what they said after her recital that day. He shivered as he remembered the afternoon, the slither of ice that slipped and dug within him when Rebecca had said, what did she say? That she had heard Briony's voice before. That was all, still she hadn't said anything more. But then his fear, his deceit had melted with the soothing of her music. She had a certain way of playing what had been played before with a new impression, a freshness of her own interpretation. He was not the only one to notice that.

They were sitting in an Italian restaurant re-shaping, evaluating their lives. It was so quick, the intrusion, the flash. They hadn't noticed anything except themselves. In retrospect Noel vaguely remembered the man – a young boy with a few soft hairs masquerading as the start of a moustache. Noel noticed him loitering. Then he had walked by their table and taken the photograph. Noel had rushed to stop him but he left, slipping through the door like a shadow, the tail of his mac struggling to keep up.

They tried to think what they had been doing; holding hands, did he have an arm around her shoulder? Thank God they hadn't kissed. Sometimes she did that or he did, although they both thought it coarse and out of place to show affection in public. But sometimes she could find herself with her cheek nudging up against his, her nose against the soft rim of his ear. Noel had been in the papers, he and other artists about to exhibit at the Tate had been interviewed. It wasn't much but enough for people to be reminded of him. They both thought the worse.

The owner of the restaurant came over to apologize, offer them a drink, liqueur, but it was too late.

'That could double the divorce settlement,' Noel tried to laugh. 'I might have to move in with you. Could you take that?'

'Could you work', said Briony, 'with the piano? With me practising all day long?' It all seemed real discussing practicalities.

They had arranged to wait a few more weeks, until after the exhibition. Noel had another painting to finish. Perhaps they wouldn't have that long, events were taking plans out of their hands.

They walked most of the way back to her flat, looking in shop windows. Before they had shied away from domestic temptations and trinkets, but now they pictured buying them together for the same house. Noel unlocked the door as if he already lived there, he opened the fridge, boiled the kettle with unusual familiarity. He went into the bedroom and she followed. It was just as she'd left it, the bed unmade, the curtains partly open caught around the windowsill as they whisked in the breeze, the telephone lying submerged in a crumpled sheet. They sat for a moment on the edge savouring the silence within the mesmerizing hum of traffic until Noel clumsily put his arms around her. It was a shame, Briony thought, that she could not sign his cast.

THIRTY-FOUR

The portrait of Briony was standing up against the wall. It was abstract enough to disguise her specific features but the lines in it were from her. Not in the same way as something he might have drawn from life, but as if their times together had influenced him, become a driving force as he worked. He had been staring at an empty canvas for weeks now and today he put the first brushstroke on it. Yesterday he had seen what he wanted when Briony sat cross-legged on the bed. Her curved bare back had caught a shadow, which distorted the curvature of her spine. Now he was recreating that and giving it to the hard-lined, labour-weary face of an office worker bending over a desk. It wasn't anyone in particular, it was an archetypal employee, whose hours were nine to five with salary and perks of small remuneration. The background was grey, the grey of an English sky, the grey of concrete, the grey of the Thames, government buildings, the grey surrounding daydreams in his life.

He had shut himself away, both Briony and Rebecca far from his mind. Occasionally he thought of the answering machine, but even his closest friend did not interrupt his work. It was not the machine's fault, but it was not the same now that he knew Rebecca had crossed into his sanctuary, which is how he thought of Adolph. He had even given it a name, a thought that caused him much anxiety. Dogs had names, he couldn't see much difference when it came to it. How did Rebecca know? Had she listened to anything?

Once he had punctured the blankness of the canvas he worked

well, feeling the flow strong within him, guiding the brush. The impulses were right, his thoughts transmitting to paint. He recreated some of his sketches from Florence: the old man in the bar, his fine bone structure transposed into the life of another. The golden light of the city resurrected itself on his canvas.

Noel felt ready for the criticism and the gamble, confident of his work, knowing he was right to set himself up where the impetus could breathe. He was only ready for more, there was so much more work he wanted to do. He believed at last he was not mediocre.

For Briony the newspaper was a burglar, that had broken into her private life. Noel would get phone calls and Rebbeca would bear the consequences. It was unfair for her to know this way. Noel had told her that Rebecca knew, that she knew her voice from the answering machine. What was the answering machine doing, talking to Rebecca? There was no doubt now, or hope of playing for time. It would blow up with incongruous timing: so who would Noel take to the opening of the Tate's exhibition?

The photograph was complimentary, no closed eyes or sultry looks. They had been caught in a moment that made it quite clear there was more than friendship between them. It was a curt vicious outline. 'Could artist Noel Kenilmore be recruiting a model for his forthcoming exhibition at the Tate Gallery?' Gossip, fodder for the slime of our society, Briony thought, disappointed by the nitpicking role of paparazzi photographers and their asinine focus of priorities.

Briony had made a point of not buying a newspaper, it was Natalie who had shown her. Calum didn't say anything and the lesson had been tense. She'd have to wait for Noel to phone. What if Rebecca phoned her? The answering machine would have to cover for her, it had got her into this trouble.

They had both agreed to lock themselves into their work; each one had a deadline. Natalie was incorporating the Grovlez piece into a concert she was arranging at Wigmore Hall. It would be Briony's first public appearance. She and Calum had started to practise regularly now.

Marcus! She was seeing him that night. She hoped he wouldn't see the picture. All those people at the garden party, someone was bound to see. Marcus would be hurt; she must get to him first.

Her mind filled with a myriad of consequences, multiplying with each thought. Perhaps nobody would see, she pretended. At least she remained anonymous. Drifting to the womb within Noel's arms, she dwelled a while on the pleasures of yesterday, smiling her first smile at his plastercast love-making, the freedom of knowing they would be together, the strain bandaged around decision.

Sophia was dissecting her party, pulling away the fancy clothing and sociable conversation and putting the heart of the matter on a virgin slab.

'Darwin thinks he'll marry her. I always thought Marcus was gay. I'm not surprised, anyone with Hilary as a mother would have to be part-demented.'

Rebecca was her assistant, cutting in here and there when a silence demanded her precision.

'A delicate creature, but strong personality no doubt. She couldn't play like that without determination and discipline as well as talent.'

Her gut reaction confirmed that Briony was the root of evil in her life. But then there was this assumption of Sophia's that Marcus was to marry her. They seemed a far more likely couple than Noel and Briony. She mulled them around as a pair, Briony was so young. Yet she had felt the static between them. Perhaps that was in her imagination.

'Noel looked preoccupied, I suppose it's the exhibition at the Tate? Can he paint with that broken arm?'

Noel had disappeared. Yesterday he was gone all day, today she assumed he was in his studio.

Sophia had made another stab on a poor innocent who had the misfortune to have worn a skirt at last year's length. 'More tea?'

'Now tell me about Italy,' she said.

Rebecca understood it was not out of malice that Sophia phoned her that evening but rather curiosity. Although her comments pointed towards suspicion, she wanted to know how Briony and Noel knew each other. Now it was Rebecca who demanded an answer to that question.

She re-phrased the question many times as she sat back on her curdling anger. She was revving, treading water in neutral while she decided which direction to take. This time there could be no doubt.

Noel was hunched over his drawing board, having had the good fortune of several hours closeted in the concentration of his work. The look on her face sent an involuntary wave quivering through him. She sat down at a stool menacingly close to his painting, an arsenal of paint within easy reach. The inquisition began.

Rebecca felt her offence wain as she asked her husband how long he had been in love with another. Within the storm of mangled emotions there was a thread of conversation in and out of shrouded clichés. Neither of them had seen the photograph but it made no difference.

'She's so young.'

'It's not your fault,' he said. And then she cried and he felt a twist in his heart, knowing it was time to taste the poison he'd served up. They walked through time and reason. 'What about Tammy?' she said. Then with a sense of living punched out of her, Rebecca left him for a while to stew in the consequences of his actions.

For once he felt he owed her the suffering of his deceit, so he looked at the phone but did not use it. He felt his loyalties torn.

Marcus was always one step ahead, in thought, in work. The

evening was agonizingly long, dipped in guilt and drenched in disappointment, sprinkled with straws of hope and baked in apprehension. His rational side struggled to say nothing had changed. It was always a long shot, but in his heart he wanted her, he'd always wanted her love.

The brandy was evaporating at an alarming speed. His hair was becoming stringy from the number of times he passed his right hand through it. She noticed he bit off hangnails. He looked tired, his face was pasty and eyes hollow. Quite sinister, she thought, and followed briefly the scenario in her mind that cast him as a bank robber in a French film: the leader, who was tough, attractive, with no scruples.

She felt herself in a courtroom, waiting to be judged, but there was no right or wrong with such charged emotion. Law was for the loopholes in logic, there was no logic here to lead to a rational conclusion. She wanted to go home, but feared him more on his own. Perhaps if she could turn him around, get him out, to a restaurant where he would have to behave. Briony needed Noel, it was no good with him not here, each working alone. She owed Marcus her support. How weak he was now, hiding behind brandy, sulking, showing for once how spoiled he'd been.

They went to a small Thai restaurant where waiters were eager to please and the clientèle hid behind whispers. It could have gone either way, fortunately it calmed him. They ordered with no appetite. She shared the Sake to hold him back but as their talk went round and round she too was sucked under by its influence.

Until now Rebecca had conducted herself with perfect composure, suffering and weighing her alternatives.

'Get out,' she said to Noel when he dared leave his studio to face her. 'Get out.'

It was late and the night distorted. He had only one place to go. He hauled himself into the car hearing its engine start as a cry behind an enemy front line and pulled off into the dark.

*

Outside, through her kitchen window Rebecca saw the gravel spit as the tyres grabbed for something solid and then he was gone, the familiar sound of his wheels at once alien and final. She allowed herself to sink, collapse but there was no chair or sofa which sunk deep enough. Only Tammy sleeping upstairs stopped her clawing at the walls, throwing herself into the arms of inanimate objects as if they could give her solace.

She poured herself a sherry and tried to take each thought at a time, maintaining her dignity. Then like a rag doll she folded up, limp, into an armchair. She sobbed quiety through the pain of it all until she felt numb. For the need of a purpose she got up, and brought the telephone over. She found herself dialling the number.

'Hello this is Briony. I'm afraid I can't come to the phone right now . . .' Rebecca charged herself up, this machine was not going to put her off.

Noel had never shown up unannounced at Briony's before. He felt himself leaving his zone and entering hers, the private life of which he knew nothing. In his worst scenario he imagined her with someone and himself rejected by both women, alone and homeless in the night. He switched on the radio where Radio 2 crooned out soft, reassuring melodies. Not his type of music but he was glad it was out there, ordinary things going on, the DJ doing his job working the night shift. Rebecca had cracked, heroically. He admired her, would give her all the money and the house. He'd worked it out there wasn't going to be much left after the spoils were divided up. He felt Rebecca at home pacing like a caged animal. Strangely he felt released, he always liked driving. There was no traffic, he was warm and snug, the mechanics of driving giving him respite from it all. He found himself anxious to see the newspaper, to see if they suited each other.

*

Everything had been said. Briony found herself explaining intangibles. Marcus had confused her. It was simple, just hard to take in. She didn't love him and even, as he said, if her perception was different, she probably still wouldn't. She wanted to go home. One more drink, he insisted. They went to a club around the corner. She wanted to see him in a taxi then she would feel relieved of her duties. He was a friend, but there was not much friendship echoing through Marcus tonight.

Rebecca was quite relaxed, comfy in the armchair, her legs crossed one hand resting on her forehead the other cradling the telephone. 'I understand Noel is not the sort of man to compromise, he needs affection . . .' She had been talking to the machine for quite some time: it was good to hear what she thought spoken out loud, no one interrupting or turning the conversation to themselves. '. . . I've known about you for a long time,' she continued, 'now I almost feel I'm included.

'What is going to happen to the answering machine? It knows the most about the three of us.'

By the time she had finished, she was too tired to think, she knew she would sleep. Noel would return or stay away as she summoned, he had not planned things well at all.

The doorbell sounded sharp, piercing, carrying through the quiet of the night. She wasn't home. He felt hackles rise to cover his fear. What would he do, he was too tired to think? 'Please Briony, don't have gone by car,' he thought, fantasizing about the key taped to its bumper. He couldn't see it on the street. Sometimes she parked around the corner when the street was full. Eureka! it was there, but where was she? It was one in the morning.

*

Briony saw the lights on her flat and knew at once he was there. He heard the unmistakeable purr of a taxi and she was home. The day was unfathomable. Could they sleep, they asked each other? Could they sleep and face it all just a little bit later?

THIRTY-FIVE

Noel's painting was lying half finished in Suffolk. That was a priority with the exhibition only days away. Briony reminded him of her concert with Calum at Wigmore Hall, that was important too. Apart they could differentiate their love from their work, dividing up their time, but now together everything intermingled, work and love were precariously balanced. Their work, it was their substance, but now they found other demands on one another.

They agreed to transform the sitting room into a studio but Briony was not sure about his presence, his working there while she practised. Would he put her off? The first day he sat out of place in the space she had cleared for him. He didn't have his things, his paints, his boxes, the drawers in which he kept his colours and brushes. Years of habit unsettled him.

Last night Briony and Noel had slept with space between them. It was brief because the whirling in their minds began at dawn. They moved into each other, wondering who had initiated the space, wanting to demolish it. She wrapped herself around and around him coiling herself up and down his body. He responded with the caresses she was beginning to know so well, each of them familiar and unsure, wanting affection, lapping up reassurance. They had needed to know they were sure.

The night had left its blackness around Rebecca. Noel knew when he telephoned the next day that overnight they had become strangers. He needed his paints, his brushes, he told her, but her words fell deep in her disinterest. She didn't want him home at first, paint another picture, she told him.

Noel put down the phone and noticed the answering machine trying to get his attention.

'Did you phone last night, before you left?' said Briony.

When he told her he hadn't, she felt a sense of foreboding. It was probably a friend. She switched it on and the force of Rebecca's message reverberated around the room.

The next morning reality broke from its shell.

Rebecca changed her mind and summoned him home. She had seen a lawyer, the word 'abandonment' was incorporated into her conversation. She was not quite prepared for the disruption. If it was to be final, she was not telling Tammy alone.

'It's for the best, it won't be long now,' Noel said before he left, imposing his decision, expecting Briony to understand.

Rebecca accepted the job at the studio, she was glad of the sewing to calm her nerves. She and Noel moved like animals defending their territory. Their evenings were strained, Noel's painting became angry. A photographer came to take pictures for the catalogue. The exhibition was next week.

Every morning and each night Noel would phone Briony and once a day he talked to the machine. The machine with all its wisdom had been violated by Rebecca's call.

'I liked talking to the machine,' Rebecca had told him. He said he would get her a machine, but no, she wanted that one. 'That machine has been responsible for destroying my life.'

'Don't be ridiculous,' he told her.

But no, she said, the machine had let him build up his love for Briony, without her even being there. 'Maybe it's the machine you love most,' she said once.

He took Rebecca to the opening of the Retrospective of Contemporary British Artists. Diminishing grants for the Arts had become an issue which entered mainstream politics, so it was well-attended by the press, a generous handful of celebrities and politicians, and opened by the Queen herself. When he first saw his painting, Briony, hanging there within his colours he knew there would never be any turning back. Rebecca saw the painting and understood at once it was a different calibre of work. 'Only now when he's gone does he start to paint,' she thought, and felt a wave of insignificance peck at her. She knew his work intimately but had never seen him do anything like this before.

She saw Noel as if there was an invisible wall between them and watched the animation bestowed upon him, the critics looking for a quote. He waited until the photographs were taken and introductions passed and then told her that he was leaving, it was their last goodbye.

That was it, Rebecca thought, as she felt like a blurred object, the crowd dipping in and out of focus around her. Nobody knew her without Noel. She put a headscarf on to become inconspicuous although she felt even the wind could blow through her now. She sat on one of the benches at the top of the steps leading to the Tate. She could see the river from there and hear the noisy, constant flow of traffic. Perhaps she was glad she had known these last few months, but then only time would decipher injustice. Her frailty rested on Noel's shoulders as she left to go home and spend the first of many nights alone.

Briony was playing, he heard the music as he came up the steps and sat a moment at the top listening. He couldn't wait to be in her surroundings which now were the only thing familiar to him. When they met, they were again as they had been that first time. His hair was damp and he shook with the trembling of each nerve, he held her close but she was never close enough. His hands holding hers as if they were glass that he didn't want to blemish. She shone with the glow of a woman in love, the light behind sifted through her hair and her joy at seeing him reddened her cheeks. She closed the door locking him in, knowing he would not be leaving again.

THIRTY-SIX

At first they moved about uneasily in the flat. Together they had rearranged the furniture clearing a niche for Noel. Within a week he missed the country but not enough to seek it, so they arranged, after Briony's concert, to spend a few days away.

Briony liked to be playing the piano by nine. He was used to getting up earlier but to pull himself away from her warmth in the morning, he thought on the pleasure of such pain. Tonight he was taking her to a concert. He anticipated her every move, sitting in her seat. She would perch, he thought, her eyes wide, taking in the audience, the orchestra, the musicians' expressions, living the music.

He padded around the flat wary of entering her territory. She ate peanut butter by the gallon, that was all she had in the kitchen. He'd felt quite self-conscious stocking up in the supermarket. She had a fierce appetite for someone so small. She never had real food, unlike Rebecca: there was always food at home. He tossed the word around, it wasn't his home now.

Every morning he went for a walk along the river. Her flat was so close to the Tate that they often went in to see the paintings. It was never quite the same as the first time he had taken her there. They had walked in feeling conspicuous, but no one had turned or recognized Noel. She'd made some ridiculous remark accompanied by a huge gasp of air that caused her words to ricochet within him. They watched as people came by, some moving closer to look, others standing back, whispering light observations. They'd enjoyed their secret, no one else knowing.

Noel always wanted to go up and say: 'No, actually it's not a tree, that's a woman, with a lithe, supple body . . .' but he never did. Briony said he wanted her soul; one day he would take it, put it on his canvas and she would be left soulless.

Yesterday he met Calum and felt at once a certain sympathy between them. Nothing to get worked up about. When he heard the music he thought he understood. It was simply something he couldn't share.

In fifteen minutes, he gauged, she would stop playing and make a cup of tea. He tiptoed to the kitchen and put a teabag in a cup. Again she thought he read her mind.

Rebecca was familiar with each speck of dust, every cupboard of clothing. His clothes which were missing, his clothes which were not, hanging there disused and neglected. She noticed the dust because she seemed to have so much time to look at each piece of furniture as if in her mind she was dismantling the house to its former state, its emptiness when they first moved in. She was not exactly lonely, but tired of the idea of once again building something from nothing, starting again. How different was everything? Not much, if anything there was more certainty in her life. She was looking out of her window, aware that Noel was no longer there influencing her. Sophia had surprised her, she phoned every day, she had never liked Noel and proffered a host of eligible men. Black knight to white Queen, was how it seemed, the way she described these eligibles, purely strategic, calculated. Rebecca was glad of the distraction and the contact. Sophia included her in their lunch parties and if there were odd numbers at dinner she thought herself on the top of the list – single woman – she had become a category: single woman. Now she would tick a different box – separated not married, and then it would be different again – divorced.

Noel had been gone for two weeks. She only liked to phone if the machine answered. They didn't talk often but there were details to discuss. She was reminded of him each time her eyes fell upon something that was his. She hadn't been to the studio since he left.

It was quiet without him. Less washing, cheaper food bills, just she and Tammy sitting down to supper. She was looking out of the window and for once the sky was not grey, it was getting colder and the cold seemed to frighten the clouds away.

She took a load of ironing upstairs to the room where their suitcases still lay from the holiday. There were a few receipts, a leaflet of the *pensione* inside. There was a packet of matches from La Dolce Vita. She thought back and remembered feeling so alive that night and then Noel had been sick. Served him right.

Maybe she would be able to spend some time in Paris, she still had many friends. Get on a plane, no she couldn't. What about Tammy? Noel could look after her. She mustn't rely on Tammy, the child had enough to cope with trying to accept their separation. Rebecca found her handbag and looked in the small zip compartment. There was a napkin from the hotel wrapped around something else. She uncovered the card, Vittorio Andronetti and a phone number was printed on it. She fingered the black embossed letters and thought of how numb she was to feeling but remembered the strength of his reassurance. He was stable, respectful, unless he feigned his friendship. That didn't matter now. She didn't want respect, he would help her and better still he was the only one who didn't know Noel. She ran her hand over the card, hesitating at first and then she dialled the number. It was satisfying to think that Noel was still paying the bill.

It was the night of Briony's concert. Noel squirted on after shave which normally he didn't use. It responded to its rare release with a concentrated blast filling the room with suffocating fumes. He was dressed in a white dinner jacket with a polka dot bow-tie now drenched in the stuff. Briony tried not to let it bother her, or hurt his feelings, by telling him he bore an unmistakeable resemblance to the Michelin man. That afternoon he had his cast taken off, it had lifted his spirits. She didn't want to change his mood, he was so proud to escort her on this debut night that it didn't matter, she told herself, how he looked.

Noel had ingested her small habits, putting the key above the door frame when he came in, turning on the machine when they left.

The machine had been a source of contention. It was no longer hers, Briony said, since Rebecca had phoned. The machine had switched its allegiance. It was used to Noel phoning and now he didn't, the only person who seemed to phone was Rebecca.

It was rubbish, of course, said Noel. 'Then let's get rid of it, we don't need it any more.'

The idea of putting the machine out to pasture filled him with remorse. If only Rebecca wouldn't phone. He tried to phone her so as not to involve Briony, but Rebecca seemed to like talking to the machine. It was probably the strain. She was not herself. It would take time for things to settle. Perhaps he should give Rebecca the machine, she asked for it once. He certainly couldn't throw it out, it would be like leaving a baby on the street. He knew he was too attached to it. So was Briony, she called it little Adolphe, that was absurd. Wrap it up with a red ribbon and leave it outside, someone would claim it. No, he didn't think he could do it. What if it fell into the wrong hands?

'Come on Noel, we're doing it again.'

'What?'

'You know, talking about Adolphe.'

'Adolph.'

'The machine.' They both felt it watching them and thought to themselves, it's just a machine, but they were sure it must have felt them ganging up on it.

Noel watched the distance close between the stage door and the rostrum. He felt each step of her walk, trying to lend his nerves so she wouldn't need hers. It was long that walk; he felt for her. What a handsome couple they made, it was impossible not to think that. She was in her prime, Calum too, both promising musicians, the world at their feet. He'd grown above that, he thought. He was, well, he didn't want to take anything for granted, but he was happier than he had ever been. His work was breaking new ground, he knew it was good and he was grateful to have Briony, for as long as she would give him. Perhaps one day she would leave him for someone like Calum. For the moment they were naturally together. They still had that crazy wildness, the wild abandon which they combined so well with life's harder edge. He knew he didn't look like Marcus or Calum when he stood there in his socks and jockeys. Hideous things men's underpants. But she never looked away or pretended he looked as glorious in his nakedness as a Michelangelo statue. No. She laughed, and somehow that was all right.

If he was butter he would have melted from her warmth. He felt twenty-five again. The applause broke his wandering, some people stood up to show their appreciation, they had to do another piece. He knew the music inside out. He liked it, he'd never listened before, not the way she taught him. She looked over to him and he felt self-conscious giving her a 'thumb's up' signal. He couldn't wait to be alone with her. To watch as she curved herself into him, stretching her legs the way she did and spreading out her toes, which, if they had skin across them, would have looked webbed. He could feel her purr and the sensation of her playing the piano just for him milked his pride. Soon it would be the two of them, cocooned. It was time, he thought, for the answering machine to start a new life. He could manage without it now. He would give it away.

Flight BA 306 'Baggage in Hall' flashed on the monitor announcing arrivals.
 Rebecca saw him waiting and fell back on her judgement. Just lately it had been wavering, warping her thoughts. Thank God

she'd made the right decision. She was right to get it out of her life. He took her bag and floundered under its weight.

'What is in here?'

'It is a surprise, Vittorio.'

She watched him buckle under the weight of her luggage but made no move to help him. Her resolve flowed through the erect line of her back as she walked decisively, unnerved by the sound of her heels resounding on the airport floor. She knew Noel thought it unusual that she had wanted the answering machine. But she had no explanation for him. Rebecca wanted it far away, and this was best. She was glad it had crossed the Channel where it could start a new life, that devil incarnate.

Vittorio drove in silence to his apartment. He rigged up an adaptor and she watched him plug the vile thing in. It was not his to play with but she let him treat it as a new toy, hesitant to tell him that answering machines were old hat.

He turned it on and music filled the room. She damned the machine for the contents of its tape, recognizing the music. It was the piano *she* played at Sophia's party.

'The music, it's Rachmaninov, who is it that's playing?' Vittorio asked her.

'She's just some girl, a girl I never really knew.'